HANDBOOK
FOR
BIBLE STUDY

HANDBOOK FOR BIBLE STUDY

Grant R. Osborne

Stephen B. Woodward

BAKER BOOK HOUSE
Grand Rapids, Michigan

Contents

Contents

PART ONE

Bible Study Methods

1

Introduction

We are living in an age of unprecedented opportunity for spreading the gospel of our Lord Jesus Christ. Communication possibilities are limitless, and people are hungry for an answer to the vacuum which secular life has produced. Man as never before sees the meaninglessness and absurdity of life without absolutes, and he is searching for a solution. The onus is on us to meet this need, to proclaim the Lord of the ages so that the lost world recognizes Christ as the only solution. God has given us a unique responsibility, and we must fulfill it.

The organized church is at a critical juncture in its development. The 1960s were days of pessimism, and many young people seriously questioned the relevance and validity of the institutional church. With the recent spate of seminars and books on church growth and church renewal, however, a new spirit of optimism has appeared, and the church again seems headed for new heights. Yet we must continue to ask whether the church fulfills the pattern established in the New Testament.

John's Gospel contains a beautiful picture of privilege and responsibility in mission, a picture that has been called the "chain of revelation." Christ is the "sent One," the only revealer of the Father (14:6; 17:3, 6). The Holy Spirit is the "sent One" who reveals Christ to men (15:26; 16:8). And Jesus' followers are "sent ones" (17:18; 20:21) who reveal Him to men (15:27) through the power of the Holy Spirit (20:22). Each link in the "chain" is crucial, and has several features: (1) Each includes both privilege and responsibility; the task is sacred and the power to perform it is promised (cf. Matt. 28:18–20). (2) Each link is contained in the one below it (see especially 17:23, 26); this means that the Triune Godhead is incorporated and revealed in us. (3) Our task begins and ends with the revealed Word of God; we do not proclaim our own message but Jesus' words of life (14:26; 21:15–17).

In light of this divine imperative, we must continually examine ourselves to see whether or not we meet God's requirements. One obstacle to proclaiming God's message is the modern-day demand for experience over faith. The world has been conquered by existentialism, the philosophy which says there are no absolutes and therefore each person must grab the experience of the moment. Although we as Christians repudiate this philosophy, we often seem to proclaim subjective experience rather than propositional truth. In this age when men are searching for an anchor, the preaching and teaching in far too many churches drifts on the sea of rhetoric. Men today are hungry for the Word of God, but instead of messages which lay bare the soul with the razor-sharp edge of Scripture, we give them the dull bludgeon of a merely interesting, man-made sermon. Men are starving for the Word of God and we feed them a milk-toast message built in our heads.

The Challenge for the Church

"We need to recover for the church," says John B. Job, "the kind of passionate involvement in the Bible that has characterized its most effective days."[1] The primary responsibility of the church today is to produce men and women of the Word, "sent ones" who lead their fellow believers deeper into the truths of Scripture. Of course, many aspects of the church are crucial for proper spiritual renewal. Yet each area of church life ultimately centers on the Word of God as the final authority for the faith and conduct of the church.

Howard Snyder lists four "currents" in the church today which have produced needed ferment and change: (1) the personal evangelism movement, stressing the fulfillment of the Great Commission but often neglecting the church; (2) the church renewal movement, stressing the church's fellowship and community life but often neglecting doctrinal truth; (3) the church growth movement, stressing the necessity of numerical growth in churches but often becoming merely a "spiritual technology"; and (4) the charismatic movement, stressing spiritual gifts and the Holy Spirit's ministry in the church but often weak in solid biblical teaching.[2]

Each of these movements is built upon a key issue in the church, and each must rest upon a solid understanding and application of scriptural truth in order to avoid imbalance and excess. For that reason the root necessity in the church today is practical Bible study. The following challenges expand on this idea:

(1) *The church must become a feeder of the flock*. According to Scripture, the pastor feeds the flock of God (John 21:15–17; I Peter 5:2) and equips the saints for the work of ministering (Eph. 4:12). In many churches, however, an in-depth pulpit ministry is the first to fall by the wayside as the pastor gets more and more swamped with visitation and administrative duties. But the true "minister" of the church referred to in the Ephesians passage is every saint, not just the pastor. It is unbiblical for a pastor to allow

his congregation to place all the responsibility on him, and it is just as unbiblical for the parishioner to allow the pastor to do all the ministering.

The church today too often fosters a shallow approach to the Word. The emphasis is on experience more than truth, and much preaching lifts verses out of context and forces them to fit a preconceived idea. The challenge to the church is to begin giving the Word of God its proper place in the church life. It must not be made subservient to evangelism or fellowship or social activities; rather it must become the guiding principle from which these other activities are organized.

(2) *The members of the congregation must become "Berean Christians."* The people of Berea, when Paul preached to them, "received the message with all eagerness and examined the Scriptures every day to see if what Paul said was true" (Acts 17:11, NIV). Although it is refreshing to see the renewed emphasis on expository preaching in recent years, too often the stress never goes beyond the pulpit ministry. This second challenge is a necessary corollary to the first. An in-depth teaching ministry in the church (and in Bible colleges and seminaries as well) must communicate methodology as well as content. Not only must the truths of Scripture be preached from the pulpit but congregations must be taught how to search out those truths for themselves. Sermonic truth never becomes personal truth for the layman until he has "searched the Scriptures" "to see if what [the preacher] said was true."

The Roman church's failure in this area was one of the causes of the Reformation. But is the "priesthood of believers" truly practiced today? How often do "papal pronouncements" come from the pulpit which are considered *ex cathedra* by the congregation? The church must begin training students of the Word instead of producing more experience-oriented Christians with little motivation to pursue an in-depth study of Scripture. Many church splits can be traced not to doctrinal debates but to the inability of the congregations to study the options for themselves. The challenge to the church is to stress individual study of the Bible among those who believe the Bible.

(3) *Christians must gain a proper understanding of the teaching ministry of the Holy Spirit.* Many segments of the church today are characterized by an anti-intellectualism which deprecates a detailed study of the Bible. The roots of this attitude can be found at the beginning of the twentieth century, in the liberal "take-over" of seminaries and institutions of learning. As a result, the evangelical wing retreated into itself and became suspicious of any academic approach to Scripture. At the same time, many teach that the only way to study the Word is directly, with no external aids, allowing the Holy Spirit to "illuminate" the passage. This is based on a misinterpretation of John 14:26, Hebrews 8:11, and I John 2:27, and gives the impression that the Spirit never uses commentaries. If that approach to those verses is correct, however, we must conclude that pastors, also, are unnecessary. But these passages do not say that the believer must study the Bible only by himself; they say that the believer does not need an intermediary between God and himself.

The true role of the Spirit in Bible study is that of a guide (John 14:26; 16:13). As we study the Word, first by ourselves and then with external tools such as commentaries, the Spirit gives us discernment and insight, leading us to truth. Every believer— layman, preacher, or scholar—needs the insights of Bible scholars to stimulate his or her understanding of a passage.

John Wesley once received a note which said, "The Lord has told me to tell you that He doesn't need your book-learning, your Greek, and your Hebrew." Wesley answered "Thank you, sir. Your letter was superfluous, however, as I already knew the Lord

has no need for my 'book-learning,' as you put it. However—
although the Lord has not directed me to say so—on my own
responsibility I would like to say to you that the Lord does not
need your ignorance, either."[3]

(4) *The church must establish and follow biblical priorities.*
There is not enough stress on the overriding importance of Bible
study in the church. The average Christian spends very little time
studying the Word of God; if he does read the Bible he rarely discovers the actual message of the text. One result of this slipshod
approach to Scripture is "proof-texting," that is, taking a verse out
of context and using it to prove a point without considering whether or not it actually applies. The church's approach to Scripture
must instead take account of its original intent and apply it to the
contemporary situation. Neither pastor nor parishioner should
ever misuse a passage from the Bible. Any message or lesson
which does so is no longer biblical, for it is based on man's
understanding, not on God's revealed Word.

(5) *The church must motivate and discipline all believers in
studying God's Word.* Christians are unprepared for the "tedi-
ousness" of thorough Bible study. The same people who will
stand for hours in a batting cage or rub their nerves raw on the
highway to the lake every weekend will refuse to spend a half
hour studying a verse of Scripture. Because our culture is so
experience oriented, many seek an "emotion a minute" when
studying the Bible. However, anyone who digs deeply into it and
applies the tools we will discuss later (e.g., background information, parallel passages, word studies) will be spending a great deal
of time on a short passage.

The process seems tedious but the results are dynamic. There
are truths in the Bible with staggering implications which would
go forever unnoticed without a disciplined study of the passages.
Because motivation comes only when the results are personally

experienced, churches and Christian groups must stress in-depth Bible study on both the individual and corporate planes. God's Word is meant to be shared, not hoarded for oneself. For this reason, believers should study the Bible themselves and then pass the things they learn on to others in their fellowship groups.

(6) *Believers must also begin to understand and stress priorities in the Christian life.* Another problem in our modern culture is the habit of taking each experience as it comes, without organizing daily plans to maximize the quality of life. This is exactly the opposite of the biblical pattern. Paul, for one, talks about "redeeming the time, because the days are evil" (Eph. 5:16, KJV). The phrase means literally, "buying up every opportunity," that is, using every moment wisely (cf. v. 15). Therefore, it is the duty of every believer to seek "priority living." Christians must recognize the more important areas of their lives and begin to give these greater emphasis.

There are three steps to "priority living." First, the Christian should list his priorities as he knows they *should* be. For instance, the first priority is his relationship with God, the second is his family, and so on. Next, he should list his genuine priorities. Many would have to admit that their business or work is at the top of the list, and that recreation time is ahead of church.[4] The final step, then, is to list ways to make the second list conform to the first.

One of the first ways is to get to know God's Word in depth and apply it. When a Christian's life becomes organized around biblical principles gleaned for himself as a result of practical Bible study, the pieces begin to fall into place. For this reason we challenge every Christian to give God's Word first place in his or her life and to study it regularly in depth. Quality is as important as quantity, and the purpose of this book is to show how to increase the quality of time spent in the Word.

(7) *Christians must learn how to apply the Word of God properly.* In *Sharpening the Focus of the Church*, Gene A. Getz discusses what he calls the "principles of New Testament edification."[5] After explaining the necessity of both a basic and an in-depth knowledge of the Word of God, he mentions two further principles: First, that "believers must be provided with opportunities to develop capacities that go beyond knowledge," that is, spiritual wisdom, discernment, and above all the love of Christ. Second, that "believers must be provided with the sum total of experiences which will help them to get beyond the knowledge level," that is, relational Christianity. Both of these, of course, are dependent on in-depth knowledge. But knowledge in itself is not enough. For it is one thing to know the basic doctrines and principles, and quite another thing to live them. Bible study is irrelevant unless it is made practical and applied to one's personal needs.

The key is the believer's desire to be changed when studying God's Word. Many Christians attend church and study Scripture more out of a sense of duty than as a result of a "hunger and thirst for righteousness." When is the last time you prayed, "Lord, show me today areas of my life where I need to change"? After a Christian asks this question, he must make certain he is properly applying God's Word. This idea will be developed later, but let us say here that a great danger lies in applying a passage in a way it is not meant to be applied.

The danger is especially real for ministers. When a preacher or teacher twists a verse in this way, he can no longer be certain he is teaching truth. It is no longer God's Word but becomes man's interpretation. In fact, it can be a false and actually non-Christian teaching, yet be accepted wholly by a group unused to evaluating the veracity of a teacher's claims. When interpreting a passage of Scripture, therefore, the teacher must determine to ascertain the biblical writer's intention, and apply this interpretation to the life-situation of the individual and the corporate fellowship.

(8) *The church must continue to seek the true interpretation of the Bible.* It is common for a person to prefer confirmation of his ideas to truth; when he studies a particular passage, he reads into it all of his old presuppositions instead of looking for the real message. There is a constant temptation to force passages to fit one's mold rather than allow them to challenge one's previous conclusions. Ministers need to stress an openness to truth in schools and churches, to teach how to look at a passage from all angles before its meaning is decided. Although no one has a corner on truth, some churches believe there is only one way to look at a doctrine—their way. Usually, the members of the congregation are not even able to study it for themselves, for they have never been taught to do so.

There is a strong movement today toward rigid doctrinal statements which take dogmatic stands on controversial issues. These stands are often based not on the Bible's teaching but on the denomination's position. Is it possible that the church is regressing to a medieval situation where the individual can no longer challenge his church's interpretation of Scripture and still remain within it? Christians must never allow tradition to take precedence over Scripture in the church. The only way to avoid this is to stress tolerance in areas where the Bible does not speak clearly and where evangelicals remain divided. The church must allow individuals to think for themselves. Instead of ostracizing Christians if they disagree on eschatalogical issues,[6] or on the Calvinism-Arminianism debate, the church must keep the dialogue where it belongs, in its proper perspective with regard to the totality of Scripture. Ministers must teach people to think, so that they do not automatically accept whatever they are taught. This will not result in a weaker faith, for people will know what they believe rather than merely knowing what they have been told. It will also prevent church splits over such issues.

Church renewal must begin with a determination to make the Word of God central within the body of Christ. Until this occurs the church will continue to flounder in schism and in a misdirected activism which often replaces true worship and dynamic fellowship. The church does not need new methods or a retreat into the security of the local group; it needs a radical return to God's Word. The church must get back to the Bible in a new way, and this means getting *into* the Bible.

True Bible Study

What does it mean to "get into" the Bible? It is exactly this issue that will be the focus of this book. We will deal with two particular problems which hamper personal Bible study. First, many otherwise good Bible study methods are either too complex and involved for the novice or too limited for the advanced student. For this reason, chapters two, three, and four will begin on a simpler level, explain the basics, and then move on to more advanced concepts. Second, personal Bible study too often suffers from a lack of external control over the reader's presuppositions, resulting in subjective, frequently erroneous conclusions. For this reason chapters five to seven will show how to apply basic tools for biblical interpretation to the personal observations the reader has made.

This book will attempt a "multi-tier" approach to Bible study. It begins with basic observations on charting the whole, discovering major emphases, and building on these to trace the biblical author's thought-development; it then returns to a minute examination of each point the author is making. It will teach how to study the Scripture passage for oneself, and how to integrate the insights of others who have studied the passage. It will also seek to communicate a wholistic approach for the average Bible student as well as the pastor and teacher. The approach of all three to Bible study is the same; only the purpose of each differs.

Finally, note that this is a *handbook* of Bible study. This means that we wish to be practical, not only telling what to do but also showing how to do it, with specific, concrete illustrations throughout. There are two ways to do this. One is to take a certain book and work through it, as Merrill C. Tenney did in his classic *Galatians: Charter of Christian Liberty*.[7] The advantage of this is continuity of material; the disadvantage is that the reader sees only one type of biblical passage. We will use a more eclectic method, choosing passages which best fit our points and giving the reader a wider exposure. Our goal is to help the reader to do it for himself; therefore, we will ask him to attempt each passage before reading the conclusions in the book. As much as possible, we will try to indicate the process as well as the results when we work through a passage. Our purpose is not only to teach the content of the passages but also to help the reader to be able to use the same process on other Scripture passages.

Due to lack of a definite and orderly approach to Bible study, many Christians do not find their study time to be very fruitful. Some misguided study methods are well known to us all. We mention two. First is the "whimsical," or "trial and error," method. One reads some portion of the Scripture several times, records some observations, perhaps consults a commentary or two, and flavors the study with some previous knowledge. No doubt God speaks to many of His children through this procedure, but at best Bible study remains a struggle and one will collect only a few good ideas. Its strength is that it is firsthand

Bible study. Its weakness is that it fails to reach much beyond superficial observation and remains subject to the undisciplined whim of the observer.

Second is the commentary approach. After a passage is selected and read, the commentaries become the teacher. The intention to go "deeper," the thorough observation of the text, and the use of commentaries, are all admirable. But the imbalance of this procedure produces serious weaknesses. Since it is primarily secondhand learning, it may be extremely dull or even artificial; the Holy Spirit is limited in His use of the observer's own personality and talents. If the observer is a teacher, he will probably communicate to others this dullness and artificiality.

It seems appropriate here to comment on a use of the Bible which God has blessed and will continue to bless, yet which has a significant procedural limitation. We refer to the "devotional meditation approach," which may employ either the "whimsical" or "commentary" procedures described above. Indeed it is not so much a "method" as it is an objective. That objective is personal edification, achieved by focusing upon application (what the passage says *to me*) rather than observation (what the passage actually says). However, since what the text says constitutes the basis from which applications are correctly and more richly derived, there is the constant inbred danger that the devotional focus—"what it says to me"—will receive more attention (and perhaps more weight) than what the biblical author actually says. Stressing application at the expense of observation may lead to a one-sided or shallow application of the truth to one's life. While God will continue to bless "devotional meditation" and while profound truths and applications will occasionally be garnered, its limited focus creates a serious drawback. Devotional meditation is unable to produce consistently the spiritual certainty which is inseparably tied to a thorough (though not necessarily technical) acquaintance with the text, that is, with what the author actually says and means. For this reason, the Christian needs a procedure that will first take him deeper into the text, and then will help him formulate applications of the text to his own experience.

Definition and Method in Bible Study

Method, as Howard Kuist stated long ago, is largely "orderly procedure." With reference to Bible study this implies four things.[8] First, method is procedure with a purpose. The reader must focus upon what the author actually says (observation) and means. (interpretation) so that he may make this message his personal possession (application). Second, method is *orderly* procedure; that is, certain steps logically follow one another.[9] This means that the reader concentrates first on the data or evidence before he applies that evidence to himself.[10] Third, method is a mentally-directed effort, and requires that the reader's mind be trained to follow the most fruitful steps to reach the goal. Fourth, method is a definite procedure which keeps the reader on the correct road and allows him time to develop his abilities. For method is more than mere procedure; it is an art which develops with the reader's own spiritual and psychological advancement. Simply learning the mechanics does not imply that one has mastered the art and science of Bible study.

There are essentially two methods of Bible study. The reader may begin with an examination of the parts of the passage until the whole has been observed (this is an "inductive" or "analytic" approach). Facts are gathered, then a conclusion is drawn. Or, one may begin with the whole and observe how the parts fit within the whole (this is the "deductive" or "synthetic" method). The whole picture receives more emphasis than the parts. Actually, the two approaches overlap, though methodical Bible study rightly emphasizes the inductive method. Other "methods" are really variations of these two basic approaches.[11]

Firsthand Bible study is important, but as we have said, this does not rule out the value of external tools. The basic tools are as follows:

(1) *English Bible with paragraph divisions.*

(2) *English dictionary.* Expert translators choose the best English words for the original Greek or Hebrew words, but not all English-speaking people are aware of the precise English meanings.

(3) *Bible concordance.* This lists all the biblical references which contain a particular word.

(4) *Bible dictionary.* This discusses biblical words and subjects treated insufficiently or not at all in English dictionaries.

(5) *Bible atlas.* This discusses topographical and geographical matters relevant to Bible lands and times.

(6) *Commentaries.* These help the reader understand a book's background, theme, and the author's style; they provide model outlines of books and offer insight into difficult passages.

The material that follows rests upon at least two assumptions that have not yet been discussed. First, the basic unit of material for Bible study is the paragraph—a distinct group of sentences dealing with a particular point. And second, the Bible is great literature and is governed by the rules of literary composition. Learning to recognize these principles constitutes a spiritual act of worship since it leads one deeper into the mind of the Spirit who moved the men to write.

Notes

1. John B. Job, ed., *Studying God's Word* (Downer's Grove, Ill.: Inter-Varsity Press, 1972), p. 7.

2. Howard A. Snyder, *The Problem of Wineskins* (Downers Grove, Ill.: InterVarsity Press, 1976), pp. 16–17.

3. Found in William Barclay, *Fishers of Men* (Philadelphia: Westminister Press, 1966), pp. 17–18. Barclay adds, "You will find a certain type of preacher and evangelist who claims that he is entirely dependent on the Holy Spirit. It is a blasphemous thing to saddle the Holy Spirit with the blame for rambling, wearisome, and unprepared effusions" (p. 18).

4. Gordon Dahl discusses the thesis: "Our problem today is that we worship our work, work at our play, and play at our worship" in *Work, Play, and Worship in a Leisure-Oriented Society* (Minneapolis: Augsburg, 1972).

5. Gene A. Getz, *Sharpening the Focus of the Church* (Chicago: Moody Press, 1974), chap. 7, pp. 75–83.

6. Of course, the *fact* of the Lord's return is not debatable, for this is clearly taught in Scripture. Christians do disagree, however, about the order and nature of the events described. On this, see Grant R. Osborne, "The 'Rapture Question,'" *Themelios* 2, no. 3 (May 1977): 77–80.

7. Merrill C. Tenney, in *Galatians: Charter of Christian Liberty* (Grand Rapids: Eerdmans, rev. ed., 1960), takes various approaches and applies each to successive portions of Galatians.

8. Howard T. Kuist, *These Words Upon Thy Heart* (Richmond: John Knox Press, 1947), pp. 59, 48.

9. Actually, the steps are so interrelated that they often overlap. For example, it is sometimes difficult to refrain from interpreting while one is observing what the text says. Yet an attempt to adhere to the logical progression is healthy, fruitful, and important for accuracy, for in the final analysis interpretation (what the text means) depends upon observation (what the text actually says).

10. The "devotional method" tends to reverse the process.

11. Unfortunately, this is not always sufficiently explained by writers, resulting in a rather bewildering number of so-called "methods" treated. For example. Merill C. Tenney, *Galatians: Charter of Christian Liberty* (Grand Rapids: Eerdmans, rev. ed., 1960) lists ten "methods"; while Howard F. Vos, who in many areas draws from Tenney's work, expands the number to sixteen. Vos's table of contents makes the apparent assumption that the inductive and synthetic methods of Bible study are but two among many. (*Effective Bible Study, A Guide to Sixteen Methods* [Grand Rapids: Zondervan, 1975], p. 14). What should have been explained is that these two are basic and the others are but variations. It is extremely unfortunate that Tenney and especially Vos imply that the "devotional method" somehow differs from the "inductive" or "synthetic" approaches (see especially Vos, p. 173).

2

Basic Methods

This chapter is organized on the premise that there are but two (often overlapping) methods of Bible study. First, we shall attempt to demonstrate what steps should be regularly followed in the synthetic or deductive process, observing the whole. This enlists the "book" or "horizontal" chart as a useful procedural aid. The Book of Jonah has been selected for demonstration. Second, by utilizing the "term" chart, we hope to demonstrate the analytic or inductive process, observing the parts. This particular device forces concentrated observation of the words ("terms") used in a passage. Jonah 1:1–3 and James 5:13–18 are used for elucidation and application.

Observing the Whole: The Book Chart

Aim and Procedural Emphasis

Seeing the whole picture protects one from distorting (by isolating) the parts which make up the whole. Thus the aim of the following procedural suggestion is to see the biblical book as a whole, to gather its central message. Though a general examination of the parts is necessary, the emphasis is deductive rather than inductive. In deductive or synthetic Bible study the parts are examined, but not in detail.

Order of the Procedure: Jonah and Eight Steps

Suppose you wished to study the Book of Jonah. How would you begin? What things would you do first, second, third, and so on until you had some insight into what God has to say? Moreover, how would you recall later what you learned? The following eight-step procedure, though not infallible, hopefully will provide most of the answers to the above questions. At first, the steps may seem somewhat mechanical. But if the reader continues to use them, they will soon become less artificial. Before we turn to a consideration of each step, we list all eight so that the procedure may be observed in its entirety. [1]

(1) Determine the historical and cultural background.

(2) Determine which type of chart best suits the material.

(3) Decide whether chapter or subject divisions should be used.

(4) Draw the chart with appropriate number of divisions.

(5) Divide chapter or subject sections into paragraph units and give each paragraph a factual title or summary description.

(6) Entitle each chapter or subject division.

(7) Complete format.

(8) Determine the author's purpose.

Application of the Procedure

(1) Determine the historical and cultural background. While the message of the book is timeless, it was written in Jonah's language and from his cultural perspective. Step one helps to throw outside light upon the meaning of the book. [2] The central

question is, How does this background information help to explain the message of the book? *Smith's Bible Dictionary* informs us that Jonah was written around 750 B.C., when Jewish nationalism was flowering.[3] Nineveh had plundered Israel in the past and was hated by her. This kind of observation will play an important part in understanding the purpose of the author (step eight).

(2) Determine which type of chart best suits the length of the material.[4] There are two basic types of charts: the horizontal and the vertical. As a rule of thumb, the horizontal chart serves best for portions longer than one chapter; the vertical for one chapter or part of a chapter. Jonah, therefore, should be horizontally charted.

(3) Decide whether chapter or subject division should be used. Chapter divisions are preferred because they are the most familiar, because most Bibles are separated in chapter divisions, and because they may be changed later if need be. However, subject divisions may be necessary if the length of the book prohibits charting by chapter (a chart should be no longer than one page or sheet) or if the chapter divisions are incorrect.[5] Jonah's chapter divisions, however, are well placed.

(4) Draw the chart with the appropriate number of divisions. (See the example below with the first five steps completed.) The format should include spaces for (a) the theme, key words, and key verse(s) above the chart; (b) chapter-subject heading blocks within the chart; (c) chapter numbers written within and below at the bottom right corners; (d) background summary at the bottom of the page.

Good style comes only with practice, but the following tips will help. (a) Do not let the chart take up the whole page, but leave considerable margins. (b) Most important, print rather than write, and leave ample space between items. Otherwise, the chart

Jonah
HORIZONTAL CHART FORMAT

Theme:
Key Words:
Key Verses:

Prophet's Rebellion and Punishment			
1 God's call to preach, prophet's rebellion (1–3)			
2 God's storm, sailor's problem, Jonah found out (4–9)			
3 Sailors fear God, Jonah over-board (10–16)			
4 Wall-to-wall whale (17)			
1	2	3	4

Background: 750 B. C., age of Jewish nationalism

will appear cluttered and it will not fulfill its purpose as a visual aid.

(5) Divide the chapter or subject sections into paragraph units and give each paragraph a factual title or summary description (see example on Jonah). First, number the paragraphs and allow space in the chapter division for the number needed. Second, give each paragraph unit a title or summary description. (Titles, as a rule, do not inform as much as summary descriptions do.) The title or description of the paragraph's contents should be short (aim at five to eight words), should distinguish that paragraph from the rest, and should describe what the paragraph actually says (observation), not what it says to the observer's life (application).[6] Third, place the number of verses in the paragraph *below* the last line in the title or description (see example). Space must be left between the paragraph numbers, descriptions, and verse numbers or visual perspective is severely hampered. Step six should be completed before moving on to the next chapter.

(6) Entitle each chapter or subject division. (See the example on the following page.) The block at the top of the chart division serves as the place for the title or description. There are three reasons for this step in the procedure. First, it provides a summary of a section's contents. Second, the literary relationships between the divisions may be seen more easily. Third, the chapter or subject division titles and paragraph unit titles form a rudimentary, "automatic" outline of the entire book. The chapter titles form major points, while the paragraph descriptions serve as subpoints. As noted, steps five and six should be completed together, one chapter or subject division at a time.

(7) Complete the chart format, indicating the theme, some of the key words, and the key verses. (See example on Book of Jonah.) The author's theme should become clearer as steps 1–6

(Observing the Whole)   Jonah

Theme: God's Compassion for the Non-Jew

Key Words: Gracious, compassion, Nineveh

Key Verses: 4:2, 11

Prophet's Rebellion and Punishment	Jonah's Prayer and Release	Prophet Preaches, Nineveh Repents	Lesson in Compassion
1 God's call to preach, prophet's rebellion (1–3)	1 Jonah's Prayer: despair and faith (1–9)	1 God's second call: Jonah obeys and preaches: "forty days" (1–4)	1 Jonah resents God's compassion (1–3)
2 God's storm, sailor's problem, Jonah is found out (4–9)	2 God's fish does as it is told: Jonah is vomited out (10)	2 Nineveh Repents (5–9)	2 God's question: "Do you do well to be angry?" (4)
3 Sailors fear God, Jonah thrown overboard (10–16)		3 God does not punish Nineveh (10)	3 God's visual aid: Jonah's compassion for plant (5–8)
4 Wall-to-wall whale (17)			4 God's lesson: God's compassion for Gentiles (9–11)
1	2	3	4

Background: 750 B.C., age of Jewish nationalism   Purpose: To combat Jewish ethnocentrism

are finished. If not, a commentary or other source can be consulted for assistance. Key words are those which are significant to the theme, usually repeated by the author. "Compassion" (4:1, 10), "Nineveh" (1:2, 3:2, passim), "Jonah," "God," "Lord," are key words in the Book of Jonah. The main idea in Jonah is God's compassion for Nineveh. The key verses are 4:2, 11, which characterize God's lovingkindness for Nineveh, a city of 120,000 non-Jews.

(8) Determine the author's purpose. While the author may clearly elucidate the theme, his reason for *selecting* the theme is not always obvious. It is important to ask why the writer choose that particular theme. Sometimes, as with the Book of Jonah, step one throws light upon the answer. In this way one may look within the book itself for clues or even outright statements of the author's purpose. We learned that Jonah lived in a day of Jewish nationalism, when disdain for non-Jews ran high. Indeed, throughout the Book of Jonah the writer contrasts Jewish narrowness (in the person of Jonah) with God's universal compassion to the non-Jew (Nineveh). By comparing these two ideas it becomes apparent that the writer wrote to convince his Jewish readers that God also loves the non-Jew and that the Jews should abort their racial provincialism. This purpose may be written at the bottom of the chart next to the "background" data.

Order of Procedure for a Longer Book

Earlier (step three) we noted that when a book has too many (more than five) chapters, or when the chapters are incorrectly drawn, one may have to employ subject divisions. (See the example below). The aim and procedure remains the same as for the shorter book, but there are three additional steps. First, due to

Charting the Longer Book: Transfer Chapter Divisions to Form Subject Divisions

Romans

Theme: "He who through faith is righteous shall live" (1:17)
Key Verses: 3:21; 8:1; 12:1
Key Words: justify, faith, Christ, Israel

"He who through faith is righteous"   "shall live"

2 Contending Ways	4 Life Benefits	Jew Will Live	How Righteous Shall Live
1 *From within:* "Practicing the Law" (1:18—3:20) *Verdict:* "By the Law no man will be declared righteous by God's measurement" -not Gentiles -not best Gentiles -not best Jews	Freedom from *wrath* "We have peace" 5 Freedom from *sin* "Sin shall not be master" 6	Present rejection? 1 Promise to those who believe (9:6–29) 2 Israel's rejection her own fault (9:30—10:21)	1 In "conformity" to new world: "living sacrifice" (12—13) -as members in Christ's body (12:3–8) -in love (12:9–21)
2 *From without:* Practicing "faith in Christ" (3:21—4:24) *Verdict:* "A man is justified by faith apart from works of Law"	Freedom from *law* "We . . . released from the Law" 7 Freedom from *death* "Free from . . . death" 8	3 Israel's rejection not final (11:1–36)	-even while in this world and under government (13:1–7) -"put on Jesus" (13:11–14) 2 Specific *issue:* Christian liberty and Christian love (14:1—15:13)
1:18 to 4:24	5 to 8	9 to 11	12 to 15:13

length of the book, several sheets of paper will be required to complete steps five and six, to entitle and describe the paragraphs and chapter divisions. Each page should contain no more than four or five chapter divisions. As the sheets are completed they may be laid side by side so that one may see the whole picture as he works toward the final one-page subject division.[7]

Second, the observer should mark the related chapters or paragraphs to indicate that they deal with the same topic within the book. Sometimes this may be fairly easy to do. At other times, however, it may be quite difficult to find just which chapters or paragraphs should be grouped together, or where the break in the book comes, or where another subject begins. Until the observer becomes familiar with the book(s), a glance at an outline given by commentators will be helpful. Commentaries by Leon Morris, John Walvoord, or others will guide the reader in his task, while firsthand examination paragraph by paragraph will protect him from slavish dependence upon the conclusions of others.

Third, chapter divisions should be transferred as subject divisions to the chart. In other words, the related groups of chapters/paragraphs should be given a *summary* description or title and placed on a horizontal subject chart. In this way the charts greatly assist the observer to grasp the whole in relation to the parts.

Observing the Parts: The Term Chart

Once the reader has the feel of the whole, he can proceed to analyze the parts in more detail. This is the inductive/analytic phase of Bible study procedure. The particular device which we shall employ is the *term chart*.

The Term and Chart: Purpose

A term is simply a word used in a characteristic way by an author. The purpose of the term chart design (see example) is to allow the observer to concentrate upon the significance of the writer's individual use of words.[8] Hopefully, this will foster the habit of careful observation. If so, the observer will find himself on the rewarding path to deeper biblical insight.

The Design's Rationale

The term chart design therefore assists the observer in four ways: (1) The chart visually sets out the biblical phrases upon which one wishes to concentrate; (2) it provides a place where observations may be recorded;[9] (3) it keeps application (what it says to me) from becoming confused with observation (what it actually says)—a deadly confusion; (4) and it provides a place for questions to be noted until one has completed the passage. Ideally, therefore, one should draw four columns for each of the above four areas. But unless the page is wider than 8½ inches (or longer than 11 inches), space does not permit. We suggest that the "Questions" and "Applications" columns be joined.

The Procedure

The procedure is relatively simply to explain and follows the term chart format. First, one selects the portion to be examined. Usually the paragraph, which constitutes a unit of thought, is the most practical. Second, beginning with column one, the observer concentrates upon the individual terms within the biblical phrase he has selected. He makes observations concerning what

TERM CHART DESIGN

Scripture	Observations	Questions/ Application
(Scripture phrases placed here)	(Observations on phrases here)	(Questions arising from observations here)

the text actually says (column two), and applies them to himself (column three). We cannot overemphasize the necessity for maintaining a clear distinction between observation and application.

Importance of Asking Questions

The key to the process is the ability to ask the right questions. [10] In this connection, Rudyard Kipling's six faithful serving men have long since proved their value and provide a good starting place:

> I have six faithful serving men,
> Who taught me all I know,
> Their names are What and Where and When
> And How and Why and Who.

In general, the six fasten upon the nature (what kind?), place, time, means (how?), and identity (whom?) of the information provided by the author.

(1) *Nature (what)*. The first question should always be, What kind of sentence is this (question, command, statement)? What does it say, mean to my life (observation–interpretation–application)? What is not said? What kind of action is described?

(2) *Place (where)*. What is the location, setting, of the book or the events described?

(3) *Time (when)*. When was it written? When was the time of the action? When will it happen (prophecy)?

(4) *Means (how)*. How is the sentence being examined related to the last? How are the ideas connected? How will action be fulfilled? How do the principles described work in my life?

(5) *Purpose (why)*. Why was it said, written, placed here?

(6) *Identity* (*who* or *whom*). Who is the writer, the audience, the characters in the book?

Finally, one should not attempt to answer time-consuming questions (recorded in column three) until the paragraph has been thoroughly scoured. To do otherwise will interrupt the observer's study of the passage. However, if the answer can be secured quickly, the observer may record the observation at once.

Old Testament Example: Jonah 1:1–3

Since Jonah was charted earlier, the general contents of its first paragraph are known and the paragraph's place within the whole is at least partially understood. We summarized the first paragraph's contents by labeling it "The Prophet's Call and Rebellion." We now turn to explore it in detail, by phrase or by clause. We elaborate considerably, not so much to expound the contents

Scripture	Observations	Questions/ Application
The word of the Lord came	Statement of fact Prophetic phrase (see concordance)	
to Jonah	Recipient of prophecy He was a *prophet* (3: 4, chart), *A Jewish nationalist* (see chart, 4:2)	Where else in Bible is Jonah mentioned? (*see Bible concordance*)
son of Amittai	*See* II Kings 14:25 (margin). Prophet to Israel, lived in Galilee (Bible atlas) in time of Jeroboam, king of Israel	Was Jonah in Galilee when he received the prophecy?

Scripture	Observations	Questions/Application
v. 2 Arise, go to Nineveh	*Command*–no choice Capital of ancient empire of Assyria (see Bible dictionary). Politically important. Destroyed 606 B.C.	Go from where?
the great city	*Special Description* Physical (3:3) "three days' walk" Numerical (4:11) "120,000 people" (Bible concordance)	Was this large for that day? Does archaeology support this? (See ar- chaeology book or Bible handbook)
cry against it	*Bad prophecy* for Nineveh, cf. 3:4, "forty days" (chart)	
wickedness		Precise meaning? Dif- ferent from "sin"? (See Bible dictionary).
before me		God is aware of earth's wicked cities Why does God let them exist? (problem of evil).
v. 3 but	*word of contrast:* Jo- nah disobeys	Why did Jonah rebel? Did Jonah lose his sal- vation? (problem of eternal security)
flee to Tarshish	Where he ran to: Long way off (see Bi- ble dictionary).	In Spain? North Africa? (Bible dictionary, atlas)
from the presence of the Lord	Geographical change of scene to escape spiritual problem (repeated in 3b)	Application to me? Why repeated?

of Jonah, but so that the reader may become familiar with the procedure.

The first clause is, "The word of the Lord came." (See chart above.) The whole sentence could have been written, adding "to Jonah," and so forth, but we wish to concentrate upon one idea at a time. Usually the first question to ask concerns the nature of the sentence as a whole. Here "the word of the Lord came" constitutes a statement rather than a question or command, and this observation is recorded in column two. "The" modifies, that is, gives additional information about, the term "word." It is a definite, particular "word," not one of many "words." The phrase "of the Lord" answers the question "whose" or "what kind of" and further identifies the "word" as belonging to "the Lord."[11] "Came" points to the fact that the "word" was not present before that time. Utilizing a Bible concordance, the observer finds that the whole clause is a kind of formula used throughout the Old Testament to introduce inspired prophecy (cf. Mic. 1:1; Zeph. 1:1; Zech. 1:1, passim.)

"To Jonah, son of Amittai" identifies the recipient of the prophecy. 'Where else in the Bible is Jonah mentioned?' is a question which will lead to further insight. This question should be recorded in column three for later perusal. "Son of Amittai" gives further information about Jonah. The NASB margin reference and Bible concordances indicate that the same description is used for Jonah in II Kings 14:25. There we learn that Jonah was a prophet to Israel who lived in Gath-hepher (later known as Galilee, as a Bible atlas will indicate). Jonah prophesied during the time of Jeroboam, king of Israel. We learned from the horizontal chart that Jonah was a Jewish nationalist and something of a racial bigot. Was Jonah in Galilee when he received the word of prophecy? The last query should be recorded in the third column on the chart, the rest in the second or "observation" column (cf. Matt. 12:39–42; parallel Luke 11:29–32). Hundreds of years later, another Prophet from Galilee would remind His Galilean listerners of Jonah of Galilee.

1:2. The terms found in the next phrase constitute a command, rather than a statement as in verse 1. A command implies that there is no choice. The next question is, How is sentence one related to sentence two? "Arise, go to Nineveh, the great city" begins the description of the contents of the prophecy; it explains just what "the word of the Lord" was when it came to Jonah. The terms "arise, go" are commands. Nineveh ("where") refers to the place Jonah is to prophesy. From a Bible dictionary or archeological sourcebook we learn that Nineveh was the capital of the ancient empire of Assyria. Nineveh was destroyed in 606 B.C., and in times past ruled Israel with cruelty. A Bible concordance informs the observer that the phrase "great city of Nineveh" is repeated by the author at 3:2, while the name "Nineveh" occurs three more times in the book (Jonah 3:2, 3:4:11). In 3:3, "three days' walk" indicates something of Nineveh's physical dimensions, while "120,000 people" (4:11) points to its large population. Three questions arise: Does "three days' walk" mean around the city or through it (there would be a vast difference in size between the two). Was 120,000 a huge population for that day? Do archaelogical discoveries support the description found in Jonah (see archaelogical sourcebook or Bible handbook)? The latter questions should be recorded in column three. (In terms of population, Nineveh was a London of the ancient world, and therefore Jonah's task was by no means insignificant.)

"Cry against it," a command, describes what Jonah is to do. "Cry" means "to prophesy with gusto," and "against it" characterizes the prophecy as one of judgment. The precise meaning of "wickedness" is a bit vague, and perhaps should be placed in the question column. How do "wickedness" and "sin" differ? (See theological dictionary). "Before me" refers to God's presence, and means that God is intimately aware of Nineveh's wickedness. An application (what it means to me, my world) or deduction which can be drawn is that God is aware of the earth's wicked cities (place in column three). "Why does God let wicked cities exist?" raises the question of the problem of evil. Though the question is ultimately insoluble, it formulates a practical dilemma for us all and is worthy of notice.

1:3a. The sentence which begins verse 3 is a statement: "But Jonah rose up to flee to Tarshish from the presence of the Lord." It is related to the previous sentence(s) in that it characterizes Jonah's response to God's command. "But" is a term of contrast and means here that Jonah does the opposite of what God orders. "Flee" answers the question, How did he disobey? "By running away." Why he disobeyed is not yet revealed (see 4:2). "Tarshish" explains *where* he ran, and should be recorded in column two. Where is Tarshish? Is it in Spain or North Africa (column three—see Bible dictionary)? In either case, it is a long way from Galilee, and in the opposite direction from Nineveh (column two—see Bible atlas). A theological question arises: When Jonah ran away did he lose his salvation? (place in column three). While neither the question nor its answer is stated in the Book of Jonah, the query may have particular interest for the observer (or perhaps for others to whom he speaks). "From the presence of the LORD" modifies "flee" and indicates a spiritual escape, in the same way that "to Tarshish" indicates a geographical escape (record in column two). The application of this observation is pertinent to modern man: Many are changing "scenery" (jobs, cities) to escape a spiritual problem (column three).[12]

1:3b. "So he went down to Joppa, found a ship which was going to Tarshish, paid the fare, and went down in it to go with them," relates to the previous sentence by focusing on the *means* Jonah used to "flee" or rebel.

New Testament Example: James 5:13-18

James 5:13-18 forms a paragraph, or group of sentences constituting a single unit of thought, and is so marked in many English Bibles (cf. NASB).[13] In view of the demonstration from the Book of Jonah, and since the James term chart below is fairly well worked out, we will limit our remarks.

5:13. "Is anyone among you suffering?" This, obviously, is a question. "Anyone" means that the question applies to all: it is a universal question. "Among you" raises the question of identity ("among whom?"), and is placed in column three. "Suffering" means "to experience injury, damage, loss, shame, or the like" (English dictionary) and this definition should be recorded in column two. The nature of this suffering ("what kind?") should be questioned (column three). In this connection, one should first discover James' use of the term elsewhere (see Bible concordance). Three verses earlier the term probably refers to suffering because one is a Christian. By using a theological wordbook, concordance, or commentary, the observer can attempt to pin down the meaning of the term "suffering" by referring to its usage elsewhere in the New and Old Testaments.

"Let him pray" is a command. There is no option (column two). It is the solution to the question just raised, which explains how it relates. But is this the only solution for Christian suffering (column 3)? "Him" refers to the sufferer (column two). Why did not James command other Christians to pray *for* him (column three)? "Pray" means "to talk to God in worship" (English dictionary, column two). Is this all that "prayer" includes (column three, see further theological dictionary)?

From the above, hopefully, four things are clear to the reader. First, the procedure begins with the sentence, and moves on to examine individually the terms within. Second, asking the right questions is vital; facility increases with practice. Third, the

TERM CHART
James 5:13–18

Scripture	Observations	Questions/ Application
Is anyone among you suffering?	Question. "Anyone" —universal question. "Suffering" means to experience injury, damage, loss, shame, or the like.	Who is "you"? (twelve Tribes, 1:1) What kind of suffering? (Physical, spiritual, emotional, all)? Some Christians suffer, cf. 5:10, OT prophets suffered. Is persecution here (suffering) for being a Christian?
Let him pray.	A command, not an option. Solution for suffering. "Him"— the sufferer prays. "Pray"—"to talk to God in worship."	Is this the only solution? How does this work? What is the relationship between suffering and prayer? What kind of prayer? What is prayer? How often should he pray? To whom?
Is anyone cheerful?	Question, universal. "Cheerful" means full of encouragement, gladness, comfort.	Why cheerful? Is it the opposite of suffering?
Let him sing praises	Command, not an option. "Sing" means to make music with the voice. "Praise" is saying that a thing or person is good.	Why is not praise spontaneous? What if you cannot carry a tune? What if you are shy? To whom do you sing? What was the importance of praise in the NT? What is its importance to me?

Scripture	Observations	Questions/ Application
v. 14 Is any among you sick?	Universal question. Is "sickness" physical? (cf. "suffering" in v. 13)	What kind of sickness? (mental, physical, emotional)
Let *him* call for the elders of the church	Command. "Him" refers to the sick one. Solution to the question. "Call"—contact the elders "Elders"—officials in the local church	Why "him" call? Why call the "elders"? Who are the "elders"?
And let *them* pray over him, having anointed him with oil, in the name of the Lord	Command, to the *elders,* not to all the Christians	What should the elders pray?
v. 15 And the prayer offered in faith	Elder's prayer. Healing prayer. Prayer of faith. "Faith"—"assurance and conviction" (Heb. 11:1)	Does sick one have to have faith? What is faith?
will restore the sick. And the Lord will raise him up	This kind of prayer heals. Does not say God heals. This is a promise. "and" connected to prayer of faith: Both needed. "Raise"— repetition of similar thought to "heal the sick"—emphasis and continuity. "Will" not "might"—definite.	How soon will sick be well? But isn't it the faith in God who heals? Does medicine heal?

Scripture	Observations	Questions/ Application
And if he has committed sins,	"And"—a new consideration. "If"—possible, not all sick meant here. Sinful sick are included.	What is sin? Not just for "holy" folk?
They will be forgiven him	Healing connected here to "forgiveness." "They" means the sins; "forgive"—to cancel the debt. "Will" is definite.	
v. 16 Therefore, confess your sins to one another	This is a command. "Therefore" points to preceding (v. 15). "Confess"—"to openly agree with God about your sin." "To one another" means public: to people (Christians)	To *all* preceding or to just "forgiveness"? Which sins should be confessed (all or some)? Who is "one another"? —*all* Christians
And pray for one another	This is a command. It is joined by "and" with "confess."	What should be prayed? Prayer for forgiveness, prayer of healing? Should all Christians pray?
So that you may be healed	This is a result clause. The healing is the result of confession and prayer.	Do you need elders?
The effective prayer	Not all prayer is effective.	What makes a prayer effective? What does effective mean? Why *effective*?

Scripture	Observations	Questions/ Application
Of a righteous man Can (do) much	This is a description of the pray-er This is a result clause. It is powerful in effect. "Much" is the extent of power.	What is a "righteous man"?
v. 17 Elijah	He was an important prophet. He was an example of power in the Lord.	Who was Elijah? (Cf. Bible dictionary and concordance)
Man, with nature like ours	He was human as we are—sinful, imperfect, weak; he loved God	Why this statement? So we too can be as powerful in prayer as Elijah?
And prayed earnestly	This is a conjunction that joins two thoughts "like us and prayed earnestly." "Earnestly" means fervently, sincerely	
That it might not rain	Purpose: no rain. His prayer was definite and appealed to supernatural.	
And it did not rain on the earth For three years and six months v. 18	Result: no rain: famine. Duration	Where was the famine? On the whole earth?
And he prayed again	"And"—conjunction which joins this verse with v. 17. "Again"—prayed a second time	What did he pray?

Scripture	Observations	Questions/ Application
And the sky poured rain And the earth produced its fruit	"and"—result: rain This is the result: fruit: *harvest.* Shows the power of his prayer.	Why is this example in this paragraph?

reader will notice that it is much easier to visualize and understand a biblical passage by means of a term chart than by following an explanation on the printed page. Fourth, following the above procedure, the observer increasingly will learn to delve into the depths of our Lord's Word, and so make richer applications to himself and to his world.

Notes

1. It is assumed that the observer will read the book through at one sitting whenever possible. Many books of the Bible require but a few minutes to do so; others, depending on the reader, take much longer. Vos, *Effective Bible Study*, pp. 26ff, suggests the following procedure: First reading—seek the theme, and discover how the author develops it, and look for a verse which sums up the theme (e.g., Gal. 2:20); second reading—further concentrate on the theme, see how it relates to different thoughts in the book, and try to determine the tone of the book (e.g., didactic [I Timothy], polemic [Galatians], paternal [Philippians]); third and forth readings—develop the outline. Tenney, in *Galatians* (p. 30), would use the third reading to discover the author's logic. Vos's and Tenney's suggestions, while admirable, are too time-consuming for most readers. Again, discovery of the outline is not as easy as both seem to imply and a commentary probably will be required. In order not to discourage the reader, this "step" is omitted from our list in the text.

2. The following sources of background information are suggested: Bible dictionaries, introductions to the Old and New Testaments, Bible encyclopedia, commentaries, Bible handbooks.

3. Some scholars hold that the Book of Jonah is a parable written as late as the fourth or fifth century B.C. by a postexilic author. Information on the various scholarly positions can be found in many Bible handbooks; for our purposes, such controversial critical questions will be laid aside.

4. There are at least four benefits of making a chart. (1) It organizes data. (2) It serves as a visual aid. The whole as well as the relation of the parts to each other can easily be seen. (3) It helps one retain what he has observed. We retain 70 percent of what we see, but only 15 percent of what we hear. (4) It conserves time. One may file a chart and use it again without redoing the whole project a year later. Charts may be employed to examine details, to summarize, to focus on key portions or concepts, and to communicate to others.

5. The rather arbitrary chapter divisions in the KJV and other English versions owe their creation in 1227 to Stephen Langton. Verse divisions were added by Robert Stephanus in 1551.

6. A good way to formulate short descriptions is to think of one word which describes the main actor, one which describes the main action, and one which summarizes the main idea of the paragraph or chapter. Such words only summarize; they should not attempt to say everything.

7. 26 of the 39 Old Testament books have less than 30 chapters and so would require less than 6 sheets (20 of the 26 have less than 15 chapters, 15 have 10 chapters or less). Isaiah, which has 66 chapters, would prove too long to lay the sheets side by side, since it would require 13 sheets. In the New Testament, the books are generally short. 17 of the 27 New Testament books or epistles have less than 6 chapters; 5 books would require 3 or less sheets of paper: Mark (16), Romans (16), I and II Corinthinas (16, 13), Hebrews (13); while another five would require 5 to 6 sheets: Matthew (28), Luke (24), John (21), Acts (28), Revelation (22). It helps to spread the sheets out on a desk or table in rows of 6 and stand up to gain a better perspective. Isaiah requires 2 rows, Matthew and Acts about a row and a half each. The observer will be surprised how much of the whole he can see.

8. Obviously, all terms are not of equal significance. However, articles such as "a," "an," and "the," while usually inconsequential, may in some cases be important. It is extremely significant that Jesus said he was "*the* good Shepherd" (John 10:11), instead of "*a* good shepherd." One should consider all terms until he develops the ability to see which are more important.

9. Observation of the facts (what the text actually says) and interpretation (what the text means) are logically distinct steps in Bible study. Although in practice they often overlap, the determination to keep them mentally apart is an important safeguard against eisegesis, that is, reading one's own ideas into the text.

10. Cf. Lloyd M. Perry and Robert D. Culver, *How to Search the Scriptures* (Grand Rapids: Baker, 1974³), pp. 226–268. Vos, *Effective Bible Study*, p. 35; Alan M. Stibbs, *Search the Scriptures* (Downers Grove, Ill.: InterVarsity Press, 1971); and Oletta Wald, *Joy of Discovery in Bible Study* (Minneapolis: Augsburg, n.d.) pp. 20–21. Wald lists five basic categories of questions to ask: explanatory; reason; implication; relationship; progress.

11. The word "LORD," printed in capitals (KJV, NASB, etc.), is used to translate the Hebrew name "Jahweh." This is the special covenant name of God revealed to Moses (Exod. 3). See the NASB preface, p. ix.

12. With reference to questions of application ("what it means to me"), the following may be suggested. What does it mean concerning (1) the world in which I live (political, social, economic, geographical); (2) my doctrine; (3) my

attitudes (toward myself, others); (4) my actions; (5) my challenges (home, walk with God, love life, school, business, etc.); (6) God's promises to me? (see Wald, *Joy of discovery*, pp. 44, 45).

13. Since there are no paragraph divisions in the original writings, modern marking can be used as guides, but need not be followed slavishly.

3

Advanced Methods

Earlier we stated that though there are variations, there are only two basic methods of Bible study: proceeding from the whole to the parts, and vice versa. This chapter builds on chapter two and seeks to accomplish two objectives: (1) to explain clearly how to diagram a passage, demonstrating the diagram's usefulness for observing the relationship between the parts; (2) to discuss and illustrate how a basic outline (for personal use, teaching, or preaching) may be obtained from the text.

Observing the Parts: Diagramming

Purpose, Definition, Value

Where the term chart focuses on individual terms, the diagram assists one to observe the relationships between the terms. Diagramming may be defined as visually rewriting the text (the paragraph) so that the grammatical parts become clearly visible. "Grammar" primarily concerns the arrangement of the words or terms within a sentence, and their relationship to each other. Aside from the value it has for easily providing an outline (see below), diagramming the text considerably helps one to extract the major thoughts in idea-packed material such as the Pauline Epistles (see Phil. 4:4–7, below).

Method: Summarized

On a piece of paper, each main statement is written on a line, with its modifiers written below the line, directly beneath the word they modify. (See example).

Particulars of the Method: Main Statements

A "main statement" consists of a group of words (terms) which (1) has a subject and verb and (2) makes complete sense when it stands alone. It is placed on the diagram at the left margin of the page.

Some sentences have two or more main statements. Some, such as I Corinthians 3:6, have three. "I planted, Apollos watered, but God was causing the growth." Each of these main statements would begin a new line on the diagram.

One does not have to be a literary genius to recognize the main statements in a sentence. First, if the observer's native language is English, he knows which words are needed for a sentence to make complete sense. "According to the grace of God which was given to me" (I Cor. 3:10) does not make complete sense until the subject, verb, and object[1] are added: "I laid a foundation." The latter phrase, however, makes complete sense on its own and "according to the grace of God . . ." is not needed. This means that "I laid a foundation" forms the main statement, while the remainder of the sentence is a modifier (more on modifiers below). One need not be a grammarian to recognize the difference in most cases. Secondly, there are words that introduce main statements. They are a clue to the observer that a main

DIAGRAMMING EXAMPLE: Jonah 1:1–3

The word . . . . .came to Jonah   (Main Statement)

   ↑of the Lord   ↑the son   (Modifiers)

                               ↑ of Amitta

(you) arise
(you) go to Nineveh

       ↑the city

         ↑great

And/ (you) cry against it

For/ wickedness has come

   ↑their   ↑up   (answers the question, "Where?",
                    ↑before me   so it is an adverb, which gives
                              more information about verbs)

But/Jonah rose

   ↑to flee   (answers the question, "Why?")

     ↑to Tarshish   (answers the question, "Where?")

     ↑from the presence

             of the Lord   (answers the question, "Whose?",

                          so it is an adjective, which can

                          only modify a noun)

So/ he went

   ↑down

   ↑to Joppa

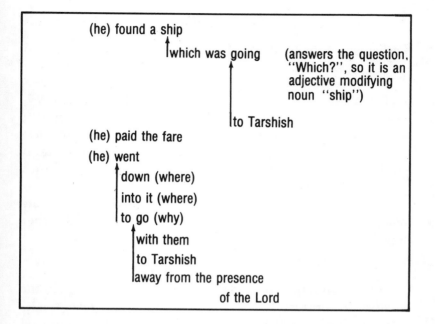

statement follows. Here is a list of twelve of the more common "tip-off" words. Ten minutes devoted to memorizing them will prevent wasted minutes later: and, but, for, so,[2] or, nor, yet, both/and, not only/but also, either/or, neither/nor, therefore (thus, for this reason, so then).

On the diagram, each of the tip-off words (conjunctions) are written in the left margin, while the main statements which they introduce begin at the margin. For example, Galatians 6:2 and 6:15:

Bear one another's burdens
and thus | (you)[3] fulfill the law of Christ
for neither | circumcision is anything
nor | uncircumcision (is anything)[3]
but | a new creation (is)[3]

Particulars of the Method: Modifiers

Modifiers are words or terms which provide additional information about other words.[4] For instance, in II Corinthians 9:7, "God loves a cheerful giver," the term "cheerful" supplies further information about the "giver." The sentence makes complete sense without it, though it does not have the same meaning. A good rule of thumb to follow is, Whatever is not needed to form a main statement is a modifier.

Modifiers have a particular place on the diagram. They are placed below the main statement and below the word(s) they modify:

God loves a giver

↑cheerful

There are two types of modifiers. These may be grouped by the *number* of words used. The first kind we may designate single-word modifiers. For example, in Ephesians 5:5, "no immoral person or impure person or covetous man . . . has an inheritance" (NASB), the terms "immoral," "impure" and "covetous" modify the words "person" and "man." They are single-word modifiers. Single-word modifiers can be adjectives, as here, and adverbs. (We shall say more later concerning how to recognize these.)

The second class of modifiers includes subordinate clauses and phrases. These, of course, contain more than a single word. The word "subordinate" (or "dependent") means that the phrase depends upon the main statement to make complete sense. A *dependent clause* is a group of words which has a subject and verb but which does not make complete sense by itself. John 2:23a, "When He was raised from the dead," has a subject "He" and verb "was raised." However, due to the introductory word "when," it *depends* upon the main statement, "His disciples remembered," to make complete sense. We provide here a list of fifteen words which indicate a subordinate (or dependent) clause modifier follows: if, although, though, that, because, since, so that, except, in ·order that, as, unless (or, lest), before, than, where, when. When these words appear in the biblical text, the observer will know that the clause which follows is dependent. It should be written below the line in the diagram, since it cannot be a main statement but it provides additional information about the main statement. Example: John 6:65

No one can come to Me (main statement)
⇧ *unless* it has been granted him (clause modifier)

A phrase is a group of words, like the clause, but unlike the clause it either has no subject or no verb. In James 5:14, "He . . . is enticed by his own lust," the latter four words, "by his own lust," constitute a phrase because there is no verb (though there is a subject). "He is enticed" makes complete sense standing alone, so these words form a main statement. The phrase, "by his own lust" (1) is a *modifier* because it is not needed for the main statement to make complete sense and (2) is a phrase because it is a group of words which has no verb.

"He . . . is enticed   (main statement)
⇧ by his own lust"   (modifier)

The following nineteen common words[5] alert the observer that a phrase-modifier is coming: by, at, in, with, for, from (out of), off, on, above, under, after, around, before, behind, between, below, over, through, of. For example, Romans 9:22:

"God . . . endured vessels
⇧ with much patience

and Romans 10:10: "man believes
⇧ with the heart

Placing the Modifier Correctly

Basically, modifiers answer one of two sets of questions. The particular set which pertains determines whether the modifier is an adjective or adverb and thus whether it is placed under a noun or under another word.[6]

Adjectives explain or reveal the following: who, whose (not, "[to] whom"), which, what kind of, how much. They modify or supply information about only nouns. Therefore, they are always placed under a term which designates a person, place, or thing, that is, a noun.

Adverbs tell: how, when, where, what is the result, why (what is the purpose). They cannot modify a noun. They can modify (1) a verb: "came *before* me" (describing "where" it came); (2) an adjective: "the *very* green couch" (describing "how" green); (3) or another adverb: "the very, very, green couch" (describing "how" very green).

The modifier's length makes no difference—whether one or ten words, whether a single word, clause, or phrase. Modifiers must be from one of the two sets of criteria. Accordingly, they must be placed under the proper term (or word). Memorization of the two sets will save considerable time later.

For example, in Jonah 1:1, the sentence reads, "The word of the Lord came to Jonah, the son of Amittai." (See above.) The main statement is made up of the minimum number of terms necessary to make complete sense, that is, a subject and verb: "The word . . . came." Therefore, all the other terms, "of the Lord," "to Jonah," and "the son of Amittai," are modifiers. "Of the Lord," though several words in length, still answers the question, "Whose?", and must therefore be placed under a noun (person, place, or thing) in the main statement.

> The word . . .[7]   came   (main statement)
> ↑of the Lord   (modifier: "whose" word?)

"To Jonah" answers the question "To whom?", or "Where?" and modifies the word "came." Therefore, it belongs to the adverb "set" of criteria and cannot modify a noun, but must modify a verb, adjective, or another adverb. Since it is obviously linked to the verb "came" (indirect object) it should be placed under that term:

   The word   came

      ↑of the Lord   ↑to Jonah (to whom? where?)

(Ideally, the phrase "to Jonah" could be written on the main statement line, since one could argue that the main statement should consist of subject, verb, and object. It makes no real difference, but the position above, it seems to us, makes the phrase's relationship to "came" very clear.) The remaining modifier, "the son of Amittai," provides further information about Jonah. "Jonah" is a noun, and therefore the phrase (because it has no verb) must be placed under "Jonah." The phrase clarifies which Jonah is meant. It reveals: "the Jonah who (which) is the son of Amittai." The passage could be diagrammed as follows:

   The[8] word . . . . . . came

      ↑of the Lord   ↑to Jonah

                   ↑the[8] son of Amittai[8] (which?, who?)[9]

Practice

Having discussed main statements and modifiers individually, let us practice diagramming them. (For a visual example of II Timothy 3:16–17, see below.) Philippians 4:6–7 provides an interesting example. "Be anxious for nothing, but in everything by prayer and supplication, with thanksgiving, let your requests be made known to God. And the peace of God, which surpasses all comprehension, shall guard your hearts and minds in Christ Jesus" (see p. 63). The first main statement is, "(You) be anxious for nothing." This constitutes the minimum number of terms neces-

DIAGRAMMING EXAMPLE
II Timothy 3:16–17

Scripture   is   inspired   (main statement)
 ↑ all   ↑ by God   (modifiers)

And/ (it is)   profitable   (understood subject and verb)
        ↑
       | for teaching
       | for reproof
       | for correction
       | for training
          ↑ in righteousness

        that/the man   may be   adequate
         ↑ of God   equipped
                          ↑ for work
                             | every
                            | good

sary to make independent sense; the subject "you" is understood. In this instance the phrase (signaled by "for") needs to be written on the line for the whole to make sense. "But" is a tip-off word that a main statement (subject, verb, sometimes object) follows. However, "in everything . . . thanksgiving," is not part of a main statement, since it is not the subject (or object) of any verb. As the tip-off words indicate ("in, by, with"), this group of words is a series of three phrases, that is, modifiers, which must be written below the main statement line (more on this shortly). But the next group of terms does contain a subject, "you" (understood); a verb, "let be made known"; and an object, "requests."

(You) be anxious for nothing   (main statement)
But/(you) let be made known requests   (main statement)
     ↑   ↑your
     ↑in everything^R (where?)
     ↑by prayer and^R supplication (how?)[10]
     ↑with thanksgiving^R (how?)
     ↑to God (to whom?)

The phrases above are adverbs, that is, they give information about a verb, adjective, or other adverb. The raised "R" signifies that the order of the phrases has been reversed for diagramming purposes, and that in the sentence, these phrases precede the main statement.

"And" signals that a third main statement follows: "peace . . . shall guard" are the fewest words needed to form a sentence which makes complete sense. "Which surpasses all comprehension" does not make complete sense by itself, so it must constitute a modifier, as does "of God," "your," and "in Christ Jesus":

    and/peace . . . . .will guard hearts/minds
     ↑the   ↑   ↑your (whose?)
     ↑of God (whose?) |in Christ Jesus
                          (where?)
    ↑which surpasses understanding (which?)
      ↑all (how much?)

There are easier passages to diagram than the one selected above, but demonstrating how the problems in this passage can be solved will help the student tackle other difficult verses. The above method is certainly not foolproof, but many, especially those whose formal knowledge of English grammar is somewhat limited, have found it to be a useful guide. If this method is faithfully practiced, the relationship between terms will often dramatically unfold before one's eyes.

The Outline

Obtaining an outline from a biblical text appears to be exceedingly difficult for many. However, this task may be greatly simplified by some knowledge of the procedure involved.

Purpose

The nature of the outline should be governed by the biblical text. Since the content of the text is ordered or arranged by the author, the outline should follow the order of the text. The author's important and less important points should be clearly distinguished by headings and subheadings. This is more easily accomplished after some knowledge of diagramming has been acquired.

Procedure

In brief, the procedure consists of four orderly steps: (1) To decide what units will be outlined: a paragraph, less than a paragraph; or, in some cases, a main topical section. (2) To determine the paragraph heading (or summary description) by referring to

OUTLINING EXAMPLE
Jonah 1:1–3
The Prophet's Call and Rebellion (Jonah 1:1–3)[12]

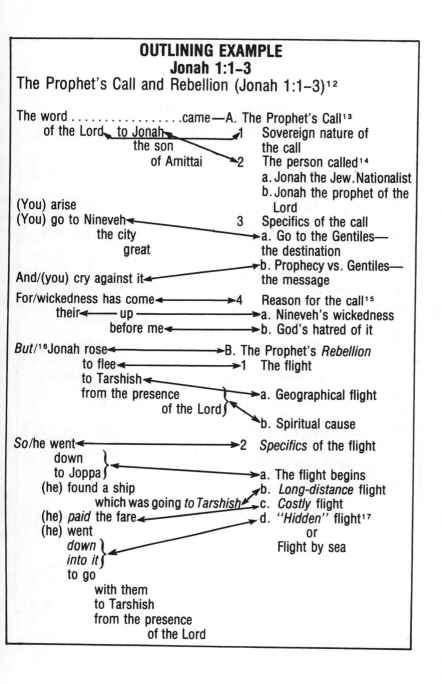

The word ....came—A. The Prophet's Call[13]
   of the Lord to Jonah   1 Sovereign nature of
         the son   the call
           of Amittai   2 The person called[14]
                         a. Jonah the Jew. Nationalist
                         b. Jonah the prophet of the
(You) arise   Lord
(You) go to Nineveh   3 Specifics of the call
      the city   a. Go to the Gentiles—
         great   the destination
                     b. Prophecy vs. Gentiles—
And/(you) cry against it   the message
For/wickedness has come   4 Reason for the call[15]
     their —— up ——   a. Nineveh's wickedness
       before me   b. God's hatred of it
But/[16]Jonah rose   B. The Prophet's *Rebellion*
     to flee   1 The flight
     to Tarshish
     from the presence   a. Geographical flight
          of the Lord
                     b. Spiritual cause
So/he went   2 *Specifics* of the flight
    down
    to Joppa   a. The flight begins
    (he) found a ship   b. *Long-distance* flight
       which was going *to Tarshish* c. *Costly* flight
    (he) *paid* the fare   d. *"Hidden"* flight[17]
    (he) went   or
      down   Flight by sea
      into it
      to go
         with them
         to Tarshish
         from the presence
            of the Lord

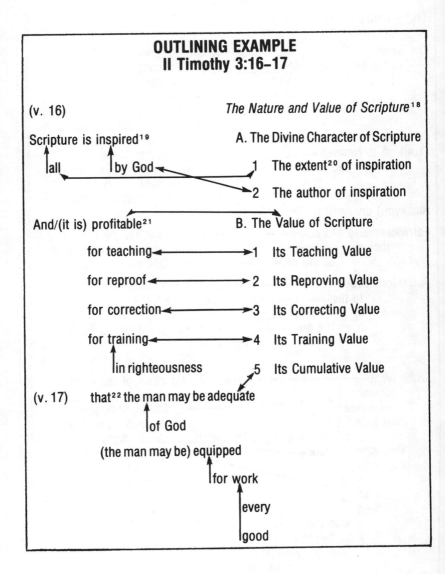

OUTLINING EXAMPLE
II Timothy 3:16–17

(v. 16)   *The Nature and Value of Scripture*[18]

Scripture is inspired[19]   A. The Divine Character of Scripture

all   by God   1 The extent[20] of inspiration

      2 The author of inspiration

And/(it is) profitable[21]   B. The Value of Scripture

for teaching   1 Its Teaching Value

for reproof   2 Its Reproving Value

for correction   3 Its Correcting Value

for training   4 Its Training Value

in righteousness   5 Its Cumulative Value

(v. 17)   that[22] the man may be adequate

of God

(the man may be) equipped

for work

every

good

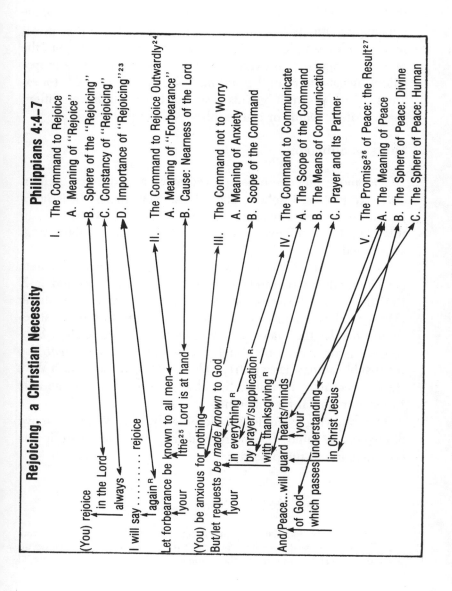

Rejoicing, a Christian Necessity

Philippians 4:4–7

I. The Command to Rejoice
    A. Meaning of "Rejoice"
    B. Sphere of the "Rejoicing"
    C. Constancy of "Rejoicing"
    D. Importance of "Rejoicing" [23]

II. The Command to Rejoice Outwardly [24]
    A. Meaning of "Forbearance"
    B. Cause: Nearness of the Lord

III. The Command not to Worry
    A. Meaning of Anxiety
    B. Scope of the Command

IV. The Command to Communicate
    A. The Scope of the Command
    B. The Means of Communication
    C. Prayer and Its Partner

V. The Promise [26] of Peace: the Result [27]
    A. The Meaning of Peace
    B. The Sphere of Peace: Divine
    C. The Sphere of Peace: Human

(You) rejoice
    in the Lord
    always
I will say . . . . rejoice
    again [R]
Let forbearance be known to all men
    |your
    |the [25] Lord is at hand
(You) be anxious for nothing
But/let requests *be made known* to God
    in everything [R]
    by prayer/supplication [R]
    with thanksgiving [R]
    |your
And/Peace...will guard hearts/minds
    |your
    of God
    which passes|understanding
    in Christ Jesus

the horizontal book chart. If none has been charted, then give the
paragraph a brief perusal and summarize its contents. (See p. 61,
note 12, for example.) (3) To formulate major headings from the
main statements. Main verbs are the key for formulating propo-
sitions or statements in the outline.[11] (See p. 61, note 13, for example.) (4) To form subpoints or subheadings from the modifiers,
that is, single words or clauses/phrases. (See p. 62.)

Hints on Subpoints

The above procedure has proved to be an extremely helpful
device to pastors, teachers, and others. Nevertheless, it is not a
perfect method and requires common sense and experience. In
this respect, the following suggestions for obtaining subheadings
are offered.

There are three areas from which subheadings may be gathered:
(1) The modifiers themselves (see p. 62, "all" and "by God"); (2)
the subjects(s), the verb, or the object in the main statement;
(3) "secondary" main statements. Usually the first main statement provides the major heading (see p. 61, "The Call"). Subsequent main statements which deal with the *same thought* also
form subheadings. (See p. 61, "The specifics of the Call.") With
these three areas in mind, the observer should always be able
to locate material for subpoints.

The following examples should prove helpful. With the above
discussion in mind, the charts and footnotes should suffice as
commentary on the procedure.

Notes

1. Though here "foundation" is the object (it receives the action) of the verb
"laid," sometimes sentences have no object of the verb's action. This occurs
when the subject does not initiate the action but is acted upon. For example, "I

laid down," and "I died" (Rom. 7:9) show the subject being acted upon. The latter form complete statements.

2. "For" and "so" are sometimes difficult to evaluate. Occasionally, both may introduce a main statement fully coordinate (independent, equal) with that which precedes. See Gal. 5:17 where the first "for" introduces a subordinate (dependent) thought. For a subordinate phrase (one that does not make complete sense by itself), see Gal. 6:17, "for I bear."

3. Understood.

4. According to Webster, a modifier is "a word, phrase, or clause that limits the meaning of another word or phrase."

5. These words, commonly known as *prepositions*, should be memorized. The preposition often begins the phrase, though there are other kinds of phrases (1) The verb phrase, which is actually a verb consisting of more than one word, such as "have been persuaded," "has loved," "will be honored"; (2) the verbal phrase, which is more complicated. See John M. Kierzek and Walker Gibson, *The Macmillan Handbook of English* (New York: Macmillan, 1960[5]), pp. 51–55. Furthermore, combinations of these tip-off words, or "group prepositions," occur: by means of, in front of, on account of, in place of, with respect to, and so on. These need not be memorized.

6. Dependent clauses may also be used as nouns. See Kierzek and Gibson, *Handbook*, pp. 58–59. As such, clauses may serve as subject, object, or appositive.

7. The ellipses not only indicate that certain words are omitted, but also may be used for spacing purposes (the terms in the main statement must be spaced to allow room for the modifiers to be written below them).

8. "The," and "of Amittai" are modifiers themselves, and thus the passage further could be broken down:

Word . . . . came
    ↑the   ↑to Jonah
  of Lord   ↑son
    ↑the   ↑the
                                ↑of Amittai

However, the degree in the text seems sufficient to make good working sense (which is the aim in this section), though it does not make for perfect grammatical analysis.

9. "The son of Amittai" is here used as an appositive. An appositive (here "Jonah" and "the son") is used "to stand for" the meaning of the other word. (Tip-off words are: namely, that is, such as, for example, for instance.) "Mr. Jones, the *salesman* of Ford Incorporated, was hurt today." The three subordinate elements to which a main statement may be reduced are dependent clause, phrase (prepositional or verbal), and appositive. See Kierzek and Gibson, *Handbook*, p. 391.

10. "And," normally a word which indicates that a main statement follows, is here used within a phrase, and so does not signal a main statement. This is an exception to the rule.

11. Linking verbs ("to be" verbs) are exceptions. The observer should look to the word following "is." This is usually an adjective.

12. The title of this paragraph is taken from the horizontal chart (p. 29), where paragraphs have already been given a description or title.

13. "The Call," the heading of this part of the outline, is gathered directly from the text by observing the *main verb*, "came."

14. The facts listed in 2a and 2b are gathered from the term chart and from the observations made in the horizontal chart.

15. "For" *in the text* indicates that an explanation or reason follows. Thus *in the outline*, the word "reason" is employed.

16. The italicized words in diagram are the rationale for the corresponding words in the outline. "But" implies that Jonah rebelled, and went contrary to the Lord's command.

17. The word "flight" is repeated in the outline to aid the reader to grasp the thread of the thought.

18. "Nature" and "value" are derived from the adjectives "inspired" and "profitable."

19. Since "inspired" is an adjective answering the question, "What kind of (Scripture)?", it focuses on the *nature* or character of Scripture. Thus the word "character" is placed in the outline.

20. "Extent" is derived from the adjective "all"—"how much?" "Author" is derived from the phrase "by God" which modifies "inspired." It indicates "*by whom*" Scripture is inspired.

21. "Profitable" fits the explanation found in note 11. It is an adjective and thus the word "value" occurs in the outline. It is important that the observer notes that the verb is "is," and causes an exception to the rule that the main verbs are keys to the main headings in the outline.

22. "That" introduces a subordinate idea. Here it refers to result, "with the result that." Thus the word "cumulative" in the outline. "That" on occasion can indicate purpose, "so that," and the like.

23. This main statement repeats the former, and thus emphsizes the importance of what has just been said. The main statement here therefore forms a subheading.

24. Philippians 4:4–7 constitutes a paragraph, that is, a group of sentences centering around a particular idea. Consult a commentary when it is difficult to see the connection in thought between sentences in the paragraph.

25. "Because" is understood; the words answer the question, "why?".

26. The term "promise" is derived from the assurance found in the word "will" in the main statement.

27. The word "result" follows from the sense of the whole paragraph.

4

More Advanced Methods

In Chapter 2, we discussed an eight-step orderly procedure for observing the whole. The procedure was based on the deductive-inductive methodological combination. In this chapter we wish to add a ninth step; and having done so, move on to discuss two important variations of the deductive-inductive methods, namely, the biographical and theological particularizations.

Laws of Composition

The ninth step involves observing the "laws of composition." The value of such a practice is two-fold. First, it considerably assists one to grasp the arrangement and so the purpose[1] of the whole; and second, it aids one to appreciate the interrelationship of the parts, and so to protect their integrity or meaning.

Definition

"Composition" refers to the author's arrangement—his "composing"—of his material. The purpose of "arrangement" is to provide unity. Just as every line and hue of a painting is ordered to advantage the whole, so in a literary composition all the parts are ordered to advantage the whole. One needs to read no farther than the first chapter or two in each of the four Gospels before he detects the different arrangements of material. Matthew begins with Jesus' family tree; John with the pronouncement of His preexistent divinity. Luke opens with the birth of John (1:5ff); Mark begins with Jesus' baptism by John. Though the facts were shared by all, each writer obviously arranged his own data or material to suit his own purpose.

Laws Defined and Listed

By "laws," we mean those constructed relationships by which the author welds a mass of data (or material) into a harmonious unity. The key word here is "relationships." These laws serve as guides, and enable one to discover the writer's purpose for so arranging his work.

We simply list here our ten "laws," to be discussed below in detail:

> comparison
> contrast
> interchange
> continuity
> continuation
> cause and effect
> progression
> cruciality
> summarization
> interrogation[2]

Though several of the laws can work in concert in a particular passage, we assume that the one which the author stresses should be considered primary. Since it is sometimes difficult to discover which law governs a passage,[3] the following descriptive paragraphs should be carefully studied.

Laws Individually Considered

(1) *Comparison.*[4] The author achieves unity by associating similar thoughts, actions, persons, and the like. The association of similar things highlights qualities which might not otherwise be obvious, or further underscores similarities. For instance, the Adam-Christ comparison (Rom. 5:12–21) highlights the universal impact of the incarnation. "For as through one man's disobedience [Adam], the many were made sinners, even so through the obedience of One [Christ], the many will be made righteous" (5:19; cf. I Cor. 15:22). Again, in Hebrews 5:1–10, the comparison between the Old Testament high priest and Christ's high priestly office calls attention to the latter. Indeed, the "as . . . so also" (5:5) structure captures the essence of the law of comparison, though the comparative words may not always be so explicit (cf. Rom. 5:6–9).

(2) *Contrast.* The law of contrast highlights the differences between two (or more) things. The light and darkness contrast in the Sermon on the Mount; the two "wineskins"; the two houses founded on contrasting foundations; the four soils with their different produce; the mighty "but now" contrast between the two ways of righteousness in Romans 3:21 (cf. 1:18—3:20) all typify the importance of this law for welding different portions of material into a harmonious whole.

(3) *Interchange.* The law of interchange is an extension of the laws of comparison and contrast. The essence of the law is *alternation*. By alternating or interchanging two or more elements (such as persons, events, ideas) their relationship is emphasized.

This occurs by each taking on "a portion of the character of the other."[5] Perhaps the most familiar example is found in Luke 1—2, where Luke interchanges John's and Jesus' early histories concerning their families, births, and prophesied futures. Traina cites the alternation of descriptions of young Samuel (I Sam. 1:1—2:11) with descriptions of the evil sons of Eli (I Sam. 2:12–17).[6] Both of these examples exhibit how alternation of the characters highlights the similarities or differences between them.

(4) *Continuity*. Another method whereby unity of material is produced is an orderly succession of reiterated elements. The relationship is established between the parts by "repetition." The elements may be terms, phrases, thoughts, or actions. Some examples are: God's repeated question to Jonah (4:4, 9); the reiterated phrase, "for three transgressions and for four," in the first two chapters of Amos (1:3, 6, 9, 11, 13; 2:1, 4, 6); the repetition of the term "love" in I Corinthians 13; the somber thrice-mentioned "God gave them over" in Romans 1 (vv. 24, 26, 28); and the reiteration of the triumphant phrase "by faith" in Hebrews 11; they all exemplify the law of "continuity"; they achieve unity through repetition. Luke's series of three parables (the lost sheep, the lost coin, and the lost son, chap. 15) provides another excellent example of how an author achieves unity through repetition.

(5) *Continuation*. The author provides unity by continuing his treatment of a chosen element (thought, action, and so on). The key to this law is "elaboration." Though it is related to continuity ("repetition"), the law of continuation *extends* rather than merely *repeats*. By this means, the author of Jonah continues his treatment of Jonah's rebellion and flight (1:1–3) in the following three paragraphs (1:4–9; 10–14; 15–17; see chart, p. 29). The author thus welds together the material contained in the first four paragraphs. See also Genesis 13 and 14, where chapter 14 continues

the account of God's blessing of Abraham (cf. 13:14–18 with 14:18); and Genesis 18—19, where the wickedness of Sodom and Gomorrah receives an extended description.

(6) *Cause and Effect.* The author often achieves harmony of the parts by moving from cause to effect, or vice versa. A reader who learns to detect this literary relationship utilized by an author is well on his way to a greatly enhanced understanding of the New Testament Epistles. Romans 5:1–11 demonstrates the cause-to-effect movement: "Therefore having been justified . . . we have peace . . . and . . . we also exult." Hebrews 1:4—2:18 illustrates how the author joins together his material (or parts) by moving from the effect (Jesus "having become as much better than the angels," 1:4) to the cause ("Jesus, because of the suffering of death [is] crowned with glory and honor," 2:9).

(7) *Progression.* By its very nature, the law of progression often involves repetition and elaboration. However, it is characterized by a significant movement from a lower point of interest to a higher. (This is often achieved by the law of cause and effect.) If the author progresses to the very highest point of concern, the result is designated, *climax.* (Similarly, musical composers often progress to a point of greater interest through the utilization of the "diminuendo-crescendo" technique.) The growing intensity of Jesus' conflict with the Pharisees (Luke 5:17—6:11) serves as an excellent example of progression. As we shall see, the author of Jonah employs this literary device from the beginning to the climactic question-answer, "Should I not have compassion on Nineveh?" (4:11).

(8) *Cruciality.* The author arranges his material so that it *pivots* around some crucial element. The key to recognizing a crucial passage is the fact that the material following the pivot always evidences a major change in direction. Several writers cite Mark 8:17–30 as the "crucial" paragraph in that Gospel. In an-

swer to Jesus' question "Who am I?" Peter replies "You are the
Messiah of God!" A decided change in Jesus' ministry occurs
following this pivotal material (cf. 8:31, "And He began to teach
them that the Son of Man must suffer"). II Samuel 11—12
provides another example: David's history takes a different course
after his infamous encounter with Bathsheba.

(9) *Interrogation.* After posing a question or problem, the
writer orders his material around the answer. For instance, the
prophet Habakkuk's questions (1:2–3) occasion God's answer in
1:5ff. Paul's acid "What shall we say then? Shall we continue in
sin that grace may abound?" (Rom. 6:1) allows him to use strong
words in response (Rom. 6:2–14, cf. 7:1, 7; 9:14, 19, 30; 11:1,
11, etc.)

(10) *Summarization.* By utilizing the law of summarization,
the author employs a synopsis (summary) preceding or following
a unit of material. Matthew 1:1ff. exemplifies the synopsis preceding the material, while Joshua 12, "Now these are the kings
which Joshua defeated," is an example of the summary following
the material.

The above ten laws serve as guides for discovering the relationships which the author established between the parts. Without
such relationships, the author's purpose would become obscured
and the full integrity of the parts rarely would be appreciated.
Though it is difficult in some cases to identify the dominant law
or relationship which the author employs, perseverance will reward the observer with rich insights into the Word of God.

Practice

Let us attempt to observe the "laws of composition" as they
apply to Jonah. The central questions before the reader are al-

ways, "Why is this paragraph or section placed here?" and "How does it relate to the others?"

According to the chart, Jonah is divided into four blocks of material, each of which is made up of two or more paragraphs. With reference to these blocks, the summary chapter headings indicate that the author progresses from a lesser interest, Jonah's rebellion, to a higher interest, a lesson in the divine compassion. Hence the major blocks of material in the Book of Jonah are arranged by the law of progression, and the individual blocks of material find their full significance only as they relate to the author's highest interest, namely, God's compassion for the non-Jew.

The chart indicates that within the blocks exist a number of paragraphs. Why are they there? How do they relate to each other? With respect to chapter one (block one), the "Prophet's Rebellion and Punishment," paragraphs one to four are related by the law of continuation. The author *elaborates* his summary statement concerning Jonah's response to God's command to preach at Nineveh. In block two, "Jonah's Prayer and Release," the first paragraph of chapter two is related to the last paragraph in chapter one by the law of cause and effect. It is no surprise that Jonah's sitting in the bowels of the Lord's great fish caused him to pray! Paragraph two lists the effect of that prayer: Jonah is released.

Notice that the author has utilized the law of cause and effect to achieve this progression.[7] That is, while the immediate subject is how Jonah's predicament causes his prayer, the larger point is that a significant change has occurred with respect to Jonah's readiness to preach. This is indicated by the words "then Jonah" (2:1; cf. "but Jonah" in 1:3).

In chapter three, the first paragraph reinforces the unity of the material of chapters 1—3 by utilizing the law of continuity or repetition; God calls Jonah the second time. The paragraph also relies on the dominant law of progression, for this time, declares the author, Jonah obeys and preaches. Paragraphs two and three record the effect of the prophetic word: Nineveh repents, God forgives. But here again, the law of cause and effect is employed to form the dominant law, progression. The author raises the level of interest from Jonah's "preaching" to a "mighty revival" among the Gentile people of Nineveh. Paragraph one in chapter four is related to the last paragraph in chapter three by the law of contrast: Jonah resents God's compassion toward Nineveh. Paragraphs two to four bring the story to its climactic close by subordinating the law of interrogation. "Do you do well to be angry?" (4:4, 9). This question allows the author to speak to prejudiced readers everywhere: "Should I not have compassion?"

For the observer not familiar with thinking in terms of these laws of composition, no doubt immediate recognition of their role is, at the very least, a bit difficult. But since the Bible is great literature, these laws are the keys to the author's purpose and to the relationship of the parts to the whole. If this is so, then it seems clear that perseverance is not too high a price to pay for a treasury of future insight.

Two Variations

Because of their signal importance to understanding Scripture, two variations of the major methods (inductive and deductive) are discussed below, namely, the "biographical" and the "theological." With reference to the importance of the biographical method, a survey of the Scriptures reveals that men are God's major visual aid for teaching and inspiration. This explains why the Bible portrays nearly three thousand separate lives, many of whose experiences reveal great spiritual lessons relevant to men and women of all generations. By means of these "biographies," abstract and often obtuse spiritual principles become concretized and thus more easily understood. With respect to the significance of the theological method, it is true that a mere grasp of the doctrines of the Bible guarantees no one the "fire" or fervor of the Holy Spirit. But it is also true that "wildfire" is usually the result of a poor grasp of the doctrines of the Scriptures. This explains why the first Christian converts were handed over to that pattern of doctrine (*didachē*, Rom. 6:17) and admonished to hold fast the faithful word which is defined or measured by the teaching (*didachē*) of sound doctrine (Titus 1:9).

The Biographical Method

Definition and Procedure

The English word "biography" stems from two Greek words, *bios*, meaning "life" and *graphein*, meaning "to write." Hence, the term "biography" means to give an account of someone's life, "to write a life" story of his character and the events and influences in his life.

The study procedure employed is a logical one:

(1) Gather the evidence or data supplied (inductive). Usually a concordance serves as the major tool. [8] The collecting should be limited at first to a single book of the Bible, if possible. Then one may move to other biblical books, and finally to whatever external source of information may lie at hand (e.g., biblical encyclopedia). The individual observations gleaned from the biblical references should be recorded on single slips of paper so that they may be easily organized.

(2) Catalogue the evidence; that is, systematize it by means of an outline (deductive). The formation of the outline may follow

or precede the collecting of evidence. Probably it is best procedure to have a model biographical outline prepared beforehand. Then the reader can slot his observations into the right section on the outline. If the need arises, the model may be supplemented (the model may also reveal what areas of a person's life have been omitted in the biblical writer's consideration). This comprehensive outline is usually designated the "biographical narrative" (see the suggested outline below).

(3) From the biological narrative outline, select the areas of the subject's life to be considered. One may wish to focus upon the *character* of the person, or one may wish to concentrate upon the major and climactic *events* of his life. In either case, the general name given to this process is "biographical exposition." Again a model outline should be constructed beforehand (see below).

(4) Relate the facts which have been gathered and catalogued to the author's overall purpose in the book. Why are these particular facts included? How do they assist the writer's presentation?[9] Why are some facts omitted?

It is hoped that the "gather, catalogue, select, relate" steps will provide the observer with an orderly path of study which will lead to rich insight.

Practice: Biographical Narrative

The aim here is comprehensive—to gather everything known about the subject from the book or elsewhere. A model outline which serves as a cataloguing tool for the facts to be gathered may be suggested:

Model

I. Heritage
   A. Ancestors
   B. Parents

C. Brothers, sisters

D. Family

E. Relatives

II. Place and Description of Birth and Death

    A. Place

        1. Importance (historically, geographically, politically)

        2. Location of

        3. Character of (city? town? business center?)

        4. Culture of

    B. Birth

        1. Significance of

        2. Unusual events

        3. Unusual or important onlookers

    C. Death

III. Childhood Advantages and Experiences

IV. Significant Events

    A. First encounter with God

    B. Conversion

    C. Call (to service)

    D. Great crisis; remedy or failure

V. Ministry/Vocation

    A. Nature

    B. Length

    C. Local

    D. Opposition

    E. Disobedience

    F. Influence (during lifetime and after)

VI. Characteristics

    A. Influences on character (home, ancestry, culture)

    B. Physical traits

    C. Positive qualities

        1. Trustworthiness

        2. Leadership

       3. Obedience
       4. Self-respect
       5. Wisdom/intelligence
       6. Courage
       7. Piety (prayer life, faith, service, other)
       8. Emotions
       9. Love
    D. Faults
       1. Untrustworthiness
       2. Pride
       3. Foolishness
       4. Impiety
       5. Emotions
       6. Selfishness
       7. Expediency
    E. Major Sin of Subject's Life
       1. Nature
       2. Steps leading to it
       3. Effect on life
VII. Relationship to Others
    A. Friends
    B. Coworkers
    C. Others
VIII. Relationship to Book: Why include (exclude) these facts about Subject?

Example: Saul

(Step 1) *Gather.* Below, the Roman numerals specify which major sections in the model outline the information fits into, while the first word designates the subsection. Then follows a brief description and the reference in I or II Samuel. Some references may fit two (or more) categories.

   I. Parent—Kish, wealthy man, I Samuel 9:2

 VI. Physical traits—tallest, most handsome in Israel, I 9:2

 VI. Positive qualities—"choice" man, I 9:2; 10:24

 IV. Call—divine to be "prince" to deliver from Philistines I 9:2—10:1

 IV. Call—anointed by Samuel, I 10:1

 IV. Call—three signs: donkeys, three men, prophecies, I 10:2–6, 11

 IV. Conversion—subsequent to call, I 10:9

 IV. Call—made public, by lot to be king, I 10:21

 VI. Positive qualities—Spirit came, changed heart, I 11:6; 10:6

 IV. Call—proverb concerning, I 10:11

 IV. Call—foretold to Samuel, I 10:15–17

 VI. Positive qualities—modest, hides among baggage, I 10:22

  V. Opposition—initial; some Jews "despise," I 10:27

  V. Opposition—magnanimous; refuses to execute, I 11

 IV. Local—first at Gibeah, I 11:4; 15:2; 15:34

  V. Opposition—wars, first, defeat Nahash, I 11

 VI. Leadership—rallies people, I 11

 IV. Call—confirmed after Nahash defeated, I 11

 VI. Positive qualities—magnanimous man of the Spirit, I 11

 IV. Call—at 40 years of age, I 13:1

  V. Length—32 years, I 13:1

  V. Opposition—wars with Philistines; stymied, afraid, offers illegal offering, I 13:9

  V. Opposition—next war with Philistines; wins, I 14:21–23

 IV. Great crisis—pressed by Philistines, disobeys, kingdom taken, I 13:8ff

 VI. Faults—does what is expedient instead of obeying, I 13:8–13

  V. Opposition—rebuked by Samuel, I 13:13f.

  V. Opposition—initial; Hebrews join Philistines, I 14:21

   V. Opposition—defeats Moab, Ammon, Edom, Zobah, Amalek, I 14:47f.

   I. Family—wife: Ahinoam, I 14:50

   I. Family—sons: Jonathan, Ishvi, Malchishua, I 14:49

   I. Family—daughters: Merab (oldest), Michal, I 18:20

 VII. Coworkers—Abner, cousin, army commander, I 14:50

 VII. Coworkers—enlists best of Israel's males, I 14:22

   V. Disobedience—spares Agag, kingdom taken, I 15:30

  VI. Faults—expedient, crafty; asks Samuel to honor him publically to save face, I 15:30

   V. Opposition—Samuel; refused to see Samuel until death, I 15:30

   V. Opposition—God; Spirit taken from him, I 16:14

   V. Opposition—evil spirit troubles, David soothes, I 16:14–23

   V. Opposition—Philistines and Goliath defeated; David grows in popularity, I 17

   V. Opposition—David anointed king by Samuel, I 16:13

 VII. Coworkers—makes David a general, I 18:5

 VII. Coworkers—jealous of David, I 18:8

  VI. Faults—uncontrollable anger; javelin at David, I 18:10 and 20:23

  VI. Faults—untrustworthy; promises Merab to David, gives to another, I 18:19

  VI. Faults—murder; slays priests; I 22:11–19

   V. Opposition—Philistines raid, I 23:27

  VI. Faults—untrustworthy, fickle, I 24:16–19 and 26:2

   V. Opposition—final wars with Philistines; killed, I 28—31

  II. Death—by Philistines, body burned, I 31

  VI. Faults—consults medium, desperate, I 31

  II. Death—David laments, II Samuel 1:17–27

   I. Family—son, Ishbosheth, made king by Abner over Israel, II 2:8

I. Family—sons, II 4:4
I. Family—concubine, II 3:7

(Step 2) *Catalogue*. Sort the slips of paper according to category and subsection. Adapt the model outline if there is an omission[10] or need for expansion. Some references will apply to more than one category.

I. Heritage
   A. Ancestors—Benjamin, I 9:2
   B. Parents—Kish, wealthy man, I 9:2
   C. Family
      1. Wife—Ahinoam, I 14:50
      2. Sons—Jonathan, Ishvi, Malchishua, I 14:49
      3. Daughters—Merab (oldest), Michal, I 18:20
   D. Relatives—Abner, cousin, general of army, I 14:49
II. Death
   A. By Philistines, body burned, I 31
   B. David laments, I 1:17–27
   C. Age 72, I 13:1
III. Significant Events
   A. Call
      1. By God, by Samuel, by people (lot), I 9:2—10:21
      2. Age 40, I 13:1
      3. Signs foretold, I 10:11
      4. Foretold to Samuel I 10:15–17
      5. Spirit comes, I 10:11; 11:6
      6. Confirmed publically again, I 11
   B. Conversion—subsequent to call; "changed heart," I 10:9
   C. Great crisis and failure—presumes office of priest, I 13:8–13

IV. Ministry/Vocation
  A. Nature—King; mandate, free Israel from Philistines, I 9:2—10:21
  B. Length—32 years, until age 72, I 13:1
  C. Opposition encountered
    1. Initial—some despised, joined Philistines, I 10:22; 14:21
    2. Wars
      a) First war defeats Nahash, Ammonite, I 11
      b) Next wars, Philistine defeated, I 14:21–23
      c) Next wars, defeats Moab, Ammon, Edom, Zobah, Amalek, I 14:47–48
      d) Goliath of Philistines, David popular, I 17
      e) Philistines continue to raid, I 23:27
      f) Final Philistine war—Saul defeated and killed, I 28—31
    3. Samuel—rebuked; dynasty taken, I 13:8–14; 15:30
    4. God—Holy Spirit taken from Saul, I 16:14
      a) David anointed king, I 16:13
      b) Kingdom taken, I 13:8–14
    5. Evil spirit troubles, David soothes, I 16:14–23
  D. Disobedience
    1. Presumed office of priest, I 13:8–14
    2. Disobeyed publicly, I 15:30
  E. Influence
    1. Loosened Philistine grip
    2. Welded people into nation, I 11:7
    3. First king
    4. Subsequently—house extinguished
V. Characteristics
  A. Physical traits—tallest, handsomest I 9:2; 10:24

B. Positive qualities
   1. At first, "choice" man, I 9:2; 10:24
   2. Modest, at first, I 10:22
   3. Good leader under Spirit's control, I 11:6
   4. Magnanimous, at first, to Jewish traitors, I 11
   5. Courage—in war, I 11:6
C. Faults
   1. Expedient, I 13:8–13; 15:30
   2. Jealous of subordinate—David, I 18:8
   3. Uncontrollable anger—javelin at David, Jonathan, I 18:10; 20:23
   4. Untrustworthy—David's promised one given to another, I 18:19
   5. Murderer—slays God's priests, I 22:11–19
   6. Fickle—David, I 24:16–19; 26:2
   7. Spiritualism consulted, I 31
D. Major sin—personal ambition
   1. Character—placed God second
   2. Steps—expedient moves
   3. Effect on life
      a) Lost kingdom of God, I 13
      b) Lost sanity?, I 16:14–23
      c) Lost life, I 31
      d) Lost dynasty, I 13
VII. Relation to Others
A. Friends—fickle
B. Coworkers—kept in family (nepotism)
   1. Abner, cousin, his general, I 14:50f
   2. David, a general, son-in-law, jealous of, tries to kill, I 18:8
   3. Enlists best men of nation, I 14:52

     C. Nation
         1. Brought some political freedom
         2. Brought unspiritual leadership
VIII. Relation to Book: Why included[11]
     A. Historically, first king of Israel
     B. People "reject" God by selection of king, I 10:19
     C. Contrast to David, God's man, I 16:7

Practice: Character Exposition

As the title indicates, this procedure focuses upon the character or qualities of a person. Major events in the subject's life are included only incidentally, that is, only as they highlight his character traits. A model outline (developed from the narrative outline) is suggested below. Data stems from that previously gathered.

Model

  I. Influences on character
     A. Home
     B. Ancestry
     C. Culture
     D. Advantages
 II. Positive qualities
     A. Trustworthiness
     B. Self-respect
     C. Wisdom and intelligence
     D. Piety (prayer life, faith, service)
     E. Emotional stability

III. Faults
  A. Untrustworthiness
  B. Pride
  C. Foolishness
  D. Impiety
  E. Emotional instability
IV. Major sin of subject's life
  A. Character of
  B. Steps leading to it
  C. Effect on subject's life
    1. immediate
    2. long-range
V. Major lesson taught by his life
  A. Positive
  B. Negative

Example: Saul

I. Influences on Character
  A. From proud ancestry—tribe of Benjamin, I Sam. 9:2
  B. Parents wealthy, I 9:2
  C. Home—assumed advantages of wealth
  D. Culture
    1. Member of God's chosen people
    2. Time of worldliness in religion (cf. Bible dictionary)
  E. Other advantages—chosen king by God and people, I 9:16
II. Positive Qualities
  A. Initially—a "choice" man, I 9:2; 10:24
  B. Initially—modest, I 10:22
  C. Excellent leader under Spirit's control, I 11:6

D. Initially—generous to enemies, I 11
E. Courageous in war, I 11:6
III. Faults
A. Untrustworthy, I 18:10
B. Fickle, I 24:16–19; 26:2
C. Impious
1. Presumed office of priest, I 13:8–14
2. Consulted medium, I 31
3. Murdered God's priests, I 22:11–19
D. Anger uncontrollable, I 18:10; 20:23
E. Jealous of subordinates, I 18:8
F. Expedient, I 13:8–13; 15:30
IV. Major sin of his life—personal amibition and expediency in action
A. Character—placed God second to own ambitions
B. Steps—ambitions produced expediency which destroyed his good qualities
C. Effect—lost everything (kingdom, sanity, life, dynasty), I 13; 16:14–23; 31
V. Major lesson taught by his life—selfish ambition and expediency are self-destructive
VI. Relation to biblical book and theme
A. Israel's desire to "replace" God with a visible king backfires, I 10:19
B. Contrast to David, a man after God's own heart, I 16:17

Practice: Biographical Event Exposition

This procedure emphasizes the major events which occur within a person's lifetime. It does not focus on his character, though that is not completely excluded. We assume that the progression of events indicates the hand of God on the subject's life. The major events mark the divisions in the outline.

Again, as above, we offer a model outline (developed from the narrative outline) to facilitate the gathering and arranging of the data. The data also comes from the narrative outline.

Model: Significant Events

  I. Birth and childhood
    A. Unusual phenomena involved
    B. Unusual persons involved
  II. Encounter with God
    A. First encounter
    B. Conversion
 III. Call to service
    A. (Unusual) phenomena and persons involved
    B. Nature and effect of call
    C. Age of subject at call
 IV. Great crisis of subject's life
    A. Remedy
    B. Failure
    C. Result
  V. Death
 VI. Relation to biblical book and theme

Example: Saul

  I. Birth to Call
    A. Birth—born to wealthy parents, I 9:2
    B. Call to be king

    1. Unusual phenomena
      a) Foretold to Samuel, I 10:15–17
      b) Accompanying signs foretold, I 10:11
      c) Spirit comes on Saul, I 10:11; 11:6
      d) Saul prophesies, I 10:11; 11:6
    2. Persons involved
      a) Called by God, I 9:2—10:21
      b) Called by Samuel, I 9:2—10:21
      c) Called (twice) by people, I 9:2—10:21
    3. Age of Saul: 40 years old; middle life,
      I 13:1
  C. Nature of call—called to be first king of Israel
    1. Called to be king, I 8:7
    2. Effect of call
      a) Loosed Israel from grip of enemies, I 11;
        14:21–23, 47–48; 17)
      b) Welded nation into one, I 11:17

II. Great crisis of Saul's life
  A. Crisis—expediency or obedience?, I 13:8–13
  B. Failure, I 13:8–13 (cf. I 15:30)
    1. Presumed the office of priest, I 13:8–13
    2. Disobeyed God's Word politically, I 15:20–31
  C. Result of failure
    1. David chosen king by God, I 16:13
    2. Kingdom taken from Saul, I 16:14; 13:8–14

III. Death
  A. Burned by Philistines, I 31
  B. David laments, II 1:17–27
  C. Age 72, I 13:1

IV. Relation to biblical book and theme
  A. Historically—crowned first king of Israel

B. Theologically—people "reject" God by selecting king
   like other nations, I 10:19; 8:7
C. Preparation for the crowning of David, I 16:17

Above we examined three elements of the biographical
method: the biographical narrative, which attempts to gather and
organize all the relevant data concerning a person; the biographical character exposition, which focuses upon the subject's personal development and qualities; and the biographical event exposition, which centers upon God's use of the person in the
events in His saving plan in history. It is hoped that the procedure
outlined above will encourage the reader to investigate God's
human visual aids.

The Theological Method

Introduction

The term *theology* simply refers to an account or teaching
(*logos*) about God (*Theos*). In the Bible, this includes His
dealings with men and the universe. A related term, *doctrine*,
concerns "that which is taught," so that one often hears of the
"doctrines" (teachings) of "theology," that is, the gathered and
ordered teachings about God and His relationship to men and the
world. Giving order to the various teachings scattered throughout
the Scriptures is the central objective of systematic theology.
Even the early church had something of a systematic theology, as
one can see from examining such passages as I Corinthians
15:1–15; 4:14–27; II Thessalonians 3:6; Romans 6:18, and others.
In the Scriptures, doctrine forms the basis for practical living;

in other words, the New Testament knows nothing of any doctrine which is not directly related to life, nor any discussion of Christian living which is not concretely tied to doctrine (cf. Rom. 6:18). Thus, in Romans, perhaps the pivotal book in the New Testament, the first eleven chapters are doctrinal (justification by faith, sanctification, Israel), and constitute the foundation for understanding the practical injunctions given in chapter 12 and following (cf. also Eph. 1—3, 4—6). Thus the view that doctrine or theology somehow stand unrelated to practical living is a view that no biblical writer would hold, and probably stems from teaching which deemphasized application to personal experience.

Definition

The theological method refers to that procedure which attempts to gather, systematize (or arrange), and relate doctrinal statements and assumptions found in the Bible or one of its books. (By "assumptions" we refer to those things which are taken for granted as true and for which there is little evidence offered; e.g., the existence of God, angels, demons). The specific aim of the theological method is to gather and arrange the major teachings mentioned within a book (or the Bible) without attempting to wring out all the minute implications of a doctrine.

Procedure

The process is similar to the biographical procedure. Indeed, apart from two preliminary steps, it is identical: gather, catalogue, relate to the whole.

(1) *Select the doctrine.* First, the student must decide which teaching he wishes to track down, and whether or not he wants to

confine his search to a book of the Bible or expand the search to the whole Bible. For example, he may wish to study a popular subject such as prayer in the Book of John, or perhaps widen the study to include all that the Bible says with reference to prayer. A book-by-book treatment seems ideal, since such a procedure will enable one to discover how God increasingly revealed to men knowledge about a subject.

(2) *Define the doctrine.* Second, the student must have a *working* idea of what he is looking for. In order for him to begin the study with some reasoned understanding against which he can measure his findings, he should refer to an external tool[12] for a definition of the doctrine. (If the definition later proves to be inadequate or faulty, it may be altered). For instance, if Paul's teaching concerning justification is selected, an initial guide would be helpful by which one could work his way through the mass of material on this doctrine. Justification may be defined as that judicial act of God by which, on the basis of the meritorious work of Christ imputed to the sinner and received by him through faith, God declares the sinner absolved from his sin, released from its penalty, and restored as righteous. Or, as the Westminster Confession of Faith states, "Justification is an act of God's free grace, wherein He pardons all our sins, and accepts us as righteous in His sight, only for the righteousness of Christ, imputed to us, and received by faith alone." If the evidence squares with the above definitions, or even if it fails to square, one has some guide to assist him in tracking down the term's meaning.

(3) *Gather the doctrine.* After selecting the doctrine and obtaining some preview of its general meaning through an external definition, the student is ready to collect the evidence.[13] It must be reiterated that the aim is not to gather *every implication* of the doctrine, but centers upon the more explicit statements of the

doctrine. The distinction between implicit and explicit will become clearer with experience; for the present, concentration upon the minutia, which tends to confuse rather than illumine the major outlines of the doctrine's meaning and application to life, should be avoided. The process of gathering may take the form of listing the data on slips of paper. Or, one may take a single sheet of paper, record the doctrine to be studied at the top, and list on the lines below the chapter and verse location, together with a brief description found in the reference. For example:

Prayer

1:1 Paul prays to the Father
1:5 Paul prays for his converts
1:8 Paul prays in agony for his converts

(4) *Catalogue the evidence.* Having gathered the evidence, it is now arranged or catalogued into a logical outline or system. (In so doing, the whole of the book's—or Bible's—teaching on the subject may be seen.) However, two problems arise.

First, it is difficult to know how and where the doctrine with which one is dealing fits in with the other major teachings of the Bible. For example, how does prayer relate to justification? Bible students have wrestled with this relational problem and have devised outlines whereby each of the major Biblical teachings can be seen and more easily understood in the light of the others. As with the biographical method, we suggest that the observer examine such a model outline before he begins his own. Of course, the model may be changed or augmented later, if need be.

Model[14]

I. Bibliology—the study of the Bible
  A. Its origin and purpose
  B. Revelation
  C. Inspiration and authority
  D. Illumination
  E. Interpretation
II. Theology proper—the study of God's triune personality
  A. Attributes
    1. Personality
    2. Omniscience
    3. Sensibility
      a) Holiness
      b) Justice
      c) Love
      d) Goodness
      e) Truth
    4. Will
      a) Freedom
      b) Omnipotence
    5. Unity
    6. Infinity
    7. Eternity
    8. Immutability (changelessness)
    9. Omnipresence
    10. Sovereignty
  B. Trinity
    1. Proof of doctrine
    2. God the Father
    3. God the Son

            a) His preexistence
            b) His names
            c) His deity
            d) His incarnation
            e) His two natures: human and divine
        4. God the Holy Spirit
            a) His personality
            b) His deity
            c) His titles
            d) Relationships
    C. Works of God (decrees[15])
        1. Creation
        2. Providence
        3. Miracles
III. Angelology—the study of angels, fallen and unfallen
    A. General facts about angels
    B. Satan
        1. Person
        2. Work
        3. Destiny
    C. Demons
        1. Personalities
        2. Work
        3. Destiny
IV. Anthropology—the study of the origin, nature and fall of man
    A. Origin
    B. Fall
    C. Sin and the sin nature
    D. True humanity restored in Christ
  V. Christology—the study of the doctrine of the Savior
    A. Preexistence

B. Incarnate existence
   1. Birth and childhood
   2. Baptism and temptation
   3. Sufferings and death
   4. Resurrection and ascension
C. Two natures (deity, humanity)
D. Present work in heaven (intercession)
E. Second coming
F. Kingdom
VI. Soteriology—the study of the doctrine of salvation
A. Election
B. Calling
C. Conversion: two elements
   1. Repentance
   2. Faith
D. Justification
E. Union with Christ
F. Adoption
G. Sanctification
H. Perseverance of the Saints
 I. Means of Grace
   1. Word of God
   2. Prayer
   3. Fellowship
VII. Ecclesiology—the study of the doctrine of the church
A. Nature: body of Christ
B. Function: forgiveness of sins
C. Government: local church
   1. Doctrine
   2. Service
   3. Ordinances
   4. Officers

D. Relationship of the New Testament church to Israel
VIII. Pneumatology—the study of the teaching of the Holy
      Spirit
      A. Names
      B. Personality and deity
      C. Symbols
      D. Ministry in the Old Testament
      E. Ministry in the New Testament
         1. To the unsaved
         2. To the saved

From the above model outline, for example, something can be gathered of the relationship between prayer and justification. Both belong to that section of the Bible's teaching that deals with the things that God has given us in our salvation (soteriology). If justification refers to our full acceptance by God for Christ's sake, then prayer must be based on this new relationship. This explains the connection in I John 1:9 between the prayer of confession and the statement that God is just to forgive the worst of us. Thus prolongation of personal guilt in prayer evidences a failure to understand how the biblical teachings on prayer and justification fit together.

After we have seen something of how the major doctrines can be arranged, a second difficulty arises. How shall we arrange the evidence when the model outline does not provide a sufficient breakdown of categories? For example, the model above provides us with the category "prayer" but does not supply any further outlining assistance for subpoints within the category. Since space prevents us from providing exhaustive outlines for each major biblical teaching, we suggest that the student simply utilize a further model found in the various works on systematic theology.[16] For instance, Henry Clarence Thiessen, in *Introductory*

Lectures in Systematic Theology (Grand Rapids: Eerdmans, 1949), pp. 395–99, offers the following outline:

1. The nature of prayer (confession, adoration, etc.)
2. The relation of prayer to providence
3. The method and manner of prayer
   a) The addresses in prayer (Father, Son, Holy Spirit)
   b) The posture in prayer
   c) The time of prayer
   d) The place of prayer
   e) Decorum in prayer
   f) The condition of the heart

Of course, everything which the Bible teaches concerning prayer is not covered in the above outline, but it is a good guideline and may be altered when the student discovers data (biblical information) which seems to demand further entries. Also, if he so desires, the student may choose to popularize those outlines whose choice of words may seem a bit archaic.

With the above points in mind, the Bible student should never be at a loss to know how to catalogue or arrange the data he discovers.

(5) *Relate the doctrine.* After a student chooses to examine a teaching within a biblical book, he must ask, How does this teaching contribute to the overall theme and purpose of the author? How does it relate to other teachings or doctrines within the book? Why are some facts about the doctrine omitted?

As an example, "The man who is just by faith shall live" forms the theme of the Book of Romans. Chapters one through four lay the foundational principle that full acceptance with God depends upon faith in Christ alone rather than upon human effort, no matter how pious the effort. (This is the doctrine of justification.) All that Paul says subsequently (cf. Rom. 5:1, "therefore") about other doctrines finds its true meaning only when related to what he has said about justification in chapters one through four. Thus, if a student majors on the doctrine of sanctification (how the believer "shall live," that is, the Christian life, chaps. 5—8, 12—15) without relating this doctrine concretely to justification, he stands in serious danger of rebuilding a system of "works" whereby what he does *earns* God's deeper fellowship with him. While this may seem fairly Christian, in reality it is a denial of the sufficiency of the work of Christ to earn the believer full acceptance and favor with God. Indeed, full acceptance with God through faith in Christ's righteousness (justification) extends throughout the entire Christian life and forms the vital nerve center of healthy Christian growth (sanctification). Thus, relating the teaching to the other doctrines in light of the author's purpose can be an eye-opener indeed, and may possibly save a lifetime of wrong thinking and experience.

Practice

We have listed and briefly discussed the five steps of the theological method procedure: select, define, gather, catalogue, relate. Now we wish to apply the procedure to a particular test case: the teaching concerning trial (temptation, suffering) in I Peter.

The doctrine of "trial" raises the question of the perseverance of the saints, a Christian issue which is aptly discussed under soteriology, that is, the study of the things which God has given us in our salvation (see the model). Since there is no further breakdown found in the model, we offer the following, based on E. G. Selwyn's discussion in *The First Epistle of Peter* (London: MacMillan and Co. Ltd., 1964), pp. 78-81.[17]

Problem of Trial

I. Suffering is according to God's will
II. Rejoicing in suffering
    1. Purges, steels, and attests the Christian's character
    2. Unites the sufferer with Christ the sufferer
    3. Prelude to the glory of the future reward
III. Sufferings/trials should not cause surprise for the Christian

We shall apply the procedure as follows.

(1) Step one. *Select.* "Trial" in I Peter

(2) Step two. *Define.* Trial is a putting to the proof by experience of good or evil. It is "generally understood as the enticement of a person (from within or without) to commit sin by offering some seeming advantage" (*Unger's Bible Dictionary*, Chicago: Moody, 1961, p. 1082).

(3) Step three. *Gather.* Below, the Roman numerals (as in the biographical model) signify the major sections given in the model outline, while the numbers in parentheses refer to the subsection. Where Roman numerals are not given, the model outline does not cover the data and will have to be augmented. References may be used more than once and in more than one category.

II.	1:6	Trials do not preclude Christian joy
	1:6	There are "various" kinds of trials
I.	1:6	Trials are "necessary," implying part of a plan
	1:6	Debilitating: trials cause "distress"
	1:6	Duration: trials are "for a little while," not forever.
II. (1)	1:7	Purpose: during trials, the genuine element of faith is separated from the ingenuine

II. (3) 1:7 Future purpose: we will be rewarded by God's ap-
             proval of our behavior on earth (praise, glory,
             honor at Christ's coming)
    1:7   Intensity: "tested by fire"
    2:15   Kinds: slander
    2:18   Kinds: "unreasonable masters" (employers)
II. (3) 2:19 Reward given
II. (2) 2:21 We "follow in Christ's steps," who suffered un-
             justly
II. (2) 2:23 Christ's behavior: did not revile
II. (2) 2:23 Christ's behavior: did not threaten
II. (2) 2:23 Christ's behavior: entrusted Himself to God
II. (2) 2:24 Christ suffered for others
    3:14   Kinds: suffer for being a Christian, slander
 I. 3:17   Better to suffer for righteousness' sake, according to
             God's will
II. (2) 3:18 Christ suffered unjustly
II. (2) 4:1 Christ suffered in flesh, so we too must suffer
    4:1   Attitude in trial: Christ suffered in flesh, we are to
             have the same purpose
II. (1) 4:1 Trials purify from sin ("ceased from sin")
    4:4   Kinds: maligned by non-believers
III. 4:12   Do not be surprised when trials come, as if things
             were out of God's control or the experience were
             uncommon
    4:12   Intensity: "fiery ordeal"
II. (1) 4:12 Purpose: "for testing"
II. (2) 4:13 Sharing the sufferings of Christ, repeated
    4:14   Kinds: "reviled" (slander)
III. (4) 4:14 We are blessed in the special work of the Spirit in
             us

4:15 Wrong kinds: let no one suffer "as a murderer, or thief, evildoer, or troublesome meddler"

II. (1) 4:17 Trial is God's judgment on His people, to purify them[18]

I. 4:19 Trial is "according to God's will," and He is a "faithful Creator"

4:19 Attitude: entrust ourselves to a faithful Creator

II. (2) 5:1 Peter witnessed the sufferings of Christ

II. (3) 5:1 Trial linked with the "glory" to come

I. 5:6 God's will: "Humble yourselves under His mighty hand"

5:6 Attitude in trial: "Humble yourselves"

5:6 Attitude: "Cast all your anxieties on Him"

I. 5:7 He cares for you, so see trials in this light

5:8 Attitude in trial: "Be sober"

5:8 Attitude: be firm in your confidence in God

III. 5:9 Same experiences as other Christians

5:10 Duration: "for a little."

I. 5:10 God of "all grace" (sufficient for every need), who "called you" (took the initiative) stands behind the Christian

5:10 Attitude: entrust ourselves to God's promise:
He will personally intervene ("Himself")
He will "perfect you"—reestablish shaken Christians
He will "confirm"—make firm in the faith
He will "strengthen"—make strong

(4) Step four. *Catalogue or arrange data.* This step was actually begun when the collecting (step three) was in process. Following the Selwyn outline, the student could file most of the data

as he went along. Where there was no suitable category, the data itself suggested new categories, for example, "4:19, Attitude: entrust ourselves to God." The major sections indicated by the Roman numerals, the subsections indicated by the numbers in parentheses (corresponding to the Selwyn outline), plus the new major sections and subsections, form the new outline. This becomes easier to formulate as one gains experience.

I. Problem of trial and God's providence
   A. There is no carefully-worked-out, exhaustive philosophy of trial (5:8b)
   B. Trials are necessary (1:6)
   C. Trials are according to God's will (3:17; 4:12, 19)
   D. God constantly cares for Christians in trial (5:6, 10)
      1. Trial must be seen against the background of God's "care" (5:6)
      2. Trial must be seen against the background of God's provision: He is sufficient for every need (5:10)
II. Nature and duration of trial
   A. Kinds of trials mentioned
      1. "Various" kinds (1:6)
         a) Slander (2:15; 4:4, 13)
         b) Unreasonable employers ("masters," 2:18)
         c) Family? (3:1–2)
         d) Due to Christian beliefs (3:14)
      2. Wrong kinds (4:15)
         a) For being a murderer
         b) For being a thief
         c) For being an evildoer
         d) For being a troublesome meddler
   B. Intensity of trial can be severe or "fiery" (1:7, 4:12)

C. Debilitating effect of trial
  1. Can cause "distress" to Christians (1:6)
  2. Can unsettle Christians (5:10)
  3. Can weaken Christians (5:10)
  D. Duration—not forever, but "for a while" (1:6; 5:10)
III. Joy under trial
  A. Trials do not preclude joy (1:6)
  B. Purpose
    1. General: "for testing" (4:12) and "judgment" (4:17)
    2. Specific: four-fold
      a) Purges, steels, and attests Christian character
        1) Genuine elements of our faith are separated from ingenuine elements (1:7)
        2) Purifies from sin (4:1)
      b) Unites the sufferer with Christ who suffered for us
        1) We "follow in His steps," who suffered unjustly (2:21; 3:18; 4:13)
        2) Christ suffered for others, so do we (2:24; 4:1)
        3) Christ's behavior under trial is our example (2:21)
          (a) He did not revile others in return (2:23)
          (b) He did not threaten others in return (2:23)
          (c) He entrusted Himself to God (2:23)
        4) Peter witnessed these sufferings of Christ (5:1)
      c) Increases personal appropriation of the work of the Spirit by the sufferer (4:14)
      d) Prelude to future reward
        1) Trial linked with the "glory" to come (5:1)
        2) Future reward of God's approval of our behavior on earth (1:7; 2:19)

IV. Proper attitude in trial
   A. Trial/suffering should not be allowed to surprise us and thus overwhelm us
      1. It is necessary to God's plan for our growth (5:12)
      2. It is the common experience of all Christians (5:9)
   B. General attitude: entrust ourselves to God (4:19)
   C. Specific attitudes:
      1. "Humble yourselves" (5:6)
      2. "Cast all your anxieties on Him" (5:6)
      3. View trials in the light of His "care" for Christians (5:6)
      4. "Be sober" (5:8)
      5. "Be firm" in confidence in God's goodness (5:9)
      6. Entrust ourselves to God's promise of assistance (5:10)
         a) He promises to personally intervene ("Himself")
         b) He promises to "perfect"—reestablish shaken Christians
         c) He promises to "confirm"—make firm in the faith
         d) He promises to "strengthen"—make strong in character

(5) Step five. *Relate doctrine to book.* The doctrine of "trial" must be seen against the background of God's sovereignty. God has called the church into being and He will maintain it in the midst of the seeming uncertainty produced by suffering and trial (1:2; 5:10). Indeed, trial is one of God's methods (4:7) for producing holiness (cf. 1:14, 15). Against this background, the goodness and faithfulness of God to His people (4:19) is considerably highlighted (5:6), and the failure or success of the perseverance of the saints is seen to be tied directly to God's care for Christians.

A student may not know the theme or the major teachings (doctrines) of a particular book (such as I Peter). A few minutes spent reading a good commentator's preface and introduction will acquaint one with the needed information. (For example, see Selwyn, pp. 64–68, 72ff.) Indeed, as has been intimated throughout Part One of this book, knowing how to utilize tools such as commentaries is of considerable value to interpretation and application. To this issue we now turn in Part Two.

Notes

1. R. G. Moulton, in *The Literary Study of the Bible* (London: Ibister and Co., 1900), remarks that "a clear grasp of the outer literacy form is an essential guide to the inner matter and spirit" (p. vi).

2. Kuist, *These Words*, pp. 80–86, following Ruskin, cites seven laws: principality-repetition; continuity-curvature (climax); radiation; contrast; interchange; consistency; and harmony. Robert A. Traina, in *Methodical Bible Study* (New York, 1957) pp. 49–52, refers to Kuist and lists sixteen laws: comparison; contrast; repetition; continuity; continuation; climax; cruciality; interchange; particularization and generalization; causation and substantiation (effect to cause); instrumentation; explanation or analysis; preparation or introduction; summarization; interrogation; and harmony. Irving L. Jensen, *Independent Bible Study* (Chicago: Moody, 1963), pp. 39–42, acknowledging his debt to Kuist, lists seven laws which he believes are the most common in biblical writings: radiation; repetition (including continuity); progression (sometimes leading to climax); contrast; climax; interchange; cruciality.

3. Traina attributes the confusing number and nomenclature to five causes: (1) the laws are closely related and therefore difficult to separate; (2) when the laws are used in combination it is difficult to see which one is primary; (3) it is difficult to categorize; (4) the nomenclature is subject to the subjective tastes of the observer; and (5) ancient and modern mind-sets differ slightly (*Methodical Bible Study*, pp. 53f.).

4. Technically, *comparison* implies that something has been examined in order to discover its similarities to *and* differences from something else. For the sake of clarity, we confine its meaning here to "the association of similar things," and reserve observation of differences for the next law, *contrast*.

5. Kuist, quoting Ruskin, in *These Words*, p. 86.

6. Traina, *Methodical Bible Study*, ad loc.

7. Cf. Kuist, *These Words*, p. 84.

8. We suggest also James Inglis, *A Topical Dictionary of Bible Texts* (Grand Rapids: Baker, 1968 [reprint]).

9. In addition to the biographical narrative and biographical exposition categories, writers sometimes include another use of biographical data. When the biographical facts are given to support or validate an author's claim, they constitute what is called the "biographical argument." Paul (Gal. 1) cites personal information to buttress his argument that his "gospel" is not man's invention.

10. In this case there is no need for section III of the model, since nothing is said of Saul's childhood.

11. Notice that the fourth step, "relate" ("gather, catalogue, select, relate"), is included in the outline itself. This is also the case in the model outlines which follow—character and event exposition.

12. Bible dictionaries, encyclopedias, church confessionals, and works of theology may be consulted. See Part Two of this book.

13. Bible concordances and topical Bibles should be utilized here.

14. This model is adapted from Lewis Sperry Chafer, *Systematic Theology* (1948), though much of the content and theological order has been changed.

15. The decrees of God have to do with His eternal purpose (Eph. 1:4; Rom. 9:22, 23)—in particular, as manifested in creation and providence.

16. There are, of course, other tools which may be considered. Whole volumes are devoted to prayer, for example; while Bible dictionaries and encyclopedias often provide good outlines which will help the reader to synthesize the data.

17. "Trial" (or suffering) also is discussed under the heading "Works of God" in Theology Proper, because it raises a question about God's preservation of His world. Thus, Selwyn entitles his discussion, "Providence and Suffering." See the model outline given above, II.C.2.

18. Commentaries should be consulted when passages are difficult to interpret.

PART TWO

Bible Study Tools

5

Basic Tools

As already discussed, there are two aspects to serious Bible study—the internal or personal study, and the external study, which involves the use of tools. Internal study consists of personal observations of the text, outlining, diagramming, and preliminary interpretation. External study adds the conclusions of others to one's own observations. These two aspects must be kept in balance in a proper Bible study. To concentrate on the internal leads to a one-sided study; the individual but confirms his or her presuppositions and reads them into the passage. To emphasize the external results in a mere collage of other people's ideas, without an integration into a wholistic study. In this case, the student simply copies comments and remains unable to properly critique the ideas. Either method, when used by itself, leads to imbalanced, often mistaken, conclusions. The two methods must act as controls for each other. The personal study provides a basis for evaluating the insights in commentaries and similar helps, and the use of external tools helps one to rethink and, when necessary, to alter his or her own conclusions. Both are crucial to a balanced study of a passage. Since the internal was the core of chapters two to four, we will center on the use of tools or study aids in the following chapters.

Principles for Developing a Library

Many think that only pastors, teachers, and churches should purchase an organized collection of works for studying the Bible. This is a mistake. While a comprehensive collection is impossible, any Bible student, lay or professional, should have a basic compilation of works to aid him in interpreting individual passages.

(1) *Purchase your library over a period of time.* The basic objection to such a collection is economic; but one need not purchase a library all at once. The cost would not be prohibitive if the works were bought one at a time, and many excellent books are not too expensive. One can still get a good Bible handbook or dictionary for less than fifteen dollars, and even a multivolume encyclopedia can be purchased for well under one hundred dollars. Commentaries, naturally, vary in price, but many are under ten dollars and some, like the Tyndale series, are less than three dollars each in paperback. As a matter of fact, more and more excellent works are coming out in paperback. If one were to space out purchases, wisely using gift opportunities such as birthdays or Christmas, a good collection would develop quickly. A student can build his library by buying commentaries on the biblical books he is personally studying at the time. Another idea is for churches to purchase many copies of a good commentary on the book the pastor is going to teach, then sell them to members at the discount price. This way the congregation is encouraged to study along with the pastor.

(2) *Make good use of the church library.* Every church would do well to develop a church library,[1] and encourage the congregation to use it. A sign of the dearth of Bible study today is the dust on commentary sections in church libraries. There should be more than one copy of important books and a good com-

prehensive selection of the more significant works in each area. Needless to say, it is impossible to be as comprehensive as some of the larger seminaries, which have collections in the hundreds of thousands. Nevertheless, a book selection policy can be maintained which will meet the needs of the congregation. Just as important is a program to educate the parishioners about the value of the library. A church should never cease motivating its people to participate in a Christian reading program. The use of book displays, book-of-the-month sections in the bulletin and church news letter, or a "library week" each year will help.

(3) *Organize your buying.* Unless one has a definite strategy in building his or her library, a collection can quickly become unbalanced. It is important to work toward a goal, perhaps one or two commentaries on each book of the Bible, several background books, the basic tools such as a dictionary or concordance, and specialty books on topics of interest such as ethics or church history. In addition, one should *plan* acquisitions, perhaps sending out a list of desired works at Christmastime and at birthdays, and planning ahead so one moves systematically toward the goal.

(4) *Always choose the better books.* We in the western world are sales conscious and are often tempted to buy the bargain rather than the quality work. This is a mistake, because in Bible study one wants quality rather than quantity. It is far better to have two good commentaries than a half dozen mediocre ones.

There are several problems with this principle: (a) It is hard to know which are the better works. Unless one has constant access to a good library, it is impossible to see, let alone use, enough commentaries to decide such a question. (We hope to suggest some of the better works throughout this study). (b) Books are constantly coming in and out of print, so many good works are difficult to locate. *Books in Print,* found in any book store, can be used to determine which books are readily available. Catalogues from major religious used book stores (see appendix for names of these) provide lists of out-of-print books. (c) Everyone has different needs and levels of ability. Many of the best commentaries presuppose a knowledge of the original languages and so are not practical for the lay student. For this reason we will in this chapter recommend works from the perspective of the lay student. (d) New works are always being published, rendering any list out of date within a short time. In our list of recommended commentaries we have tried to note any major forthcoming works of which we are aware. Cyril Barber, in his *Minister's Library*, has tried to solve this problem with a "Periodic Supplement," the first of which was published in 1976. [2] This is one way to keep up to date. However, the classics are never outdated, as may be seen in the number of works in our list which were published fifty or more years ago.

(5) *Choose works which are true to the text.* Many commentaries depart from the biblical author's intention and trace highly subjective and peripheral themes. The individual would do well to check whether an author has used the original languages (not necessarily in his discussion but rather in his research). It is surprising how many seemingly authoritative works are weak in their exegesis (see the following chapter for principles of exegesis). Such works are not useful for Bible study, for one must reject more of the data therein than he accepts. In the limited time available for Bible study, it is crucial to use works which give maximum return for time spent.

(6) *Be willing to use works with which you may not necessarily agree.* There is a tendency on the part of evangelicals to refuse to use works which do not follow evangelical presuppositions. This may be a wise course for immature Christians, but not for experienced Bible students. It must be recognized that there is no one

author with whom a student will entirely agree. A major premise in our principles for Bible study is that the student examine critically every work he uses. Every believer must follow the example of the Bereans (Acts 17; see introductory chapter), who carefully examined claims to see if Scripture supported them. The practice of demanding conformity only compounds errors, because then the reader's views are never challenged. In our bibliography, therefore, we will evaluate books for their quality, not for their adherence to predetermined views. If they depart significantly from the evangelical norm, however, we will try to note that fact.

General Study Tools

In addition to commentaries and books of special interest, there are several general tools which are required reference works for Bible study. Naturally, it is difficult to purchase all at once, and the student is recommended to establish a priority list and purchase them one at a time. For this reason, the present list of general tools is in the order of priority we would follow. Each student should, however, feel free to change the order to meet his or her needs.

(1) A good, exhaustive concordance is an essential tool. It is impossible to do word studies or trace parallel passages without a good concordance. The best is probably Robert Young, *Analytical Concordance to the Bible* (Eerdmans, 1955), which lists words according to their use in the original languages; it is an excellent tool for the nonspecialist. The other major work is James Strong, *Exhaustive Concordance of the Bible* (Baker, 1977 reprint), which is more complete but works from the English text.

A less expensive but still good work is Alexander Cruden, *Cruden's Unabridged Concordance* (Baker, 1953). Most of the later versions are finally being compiled into concordances.

(2) A good Bible dictionary or encyclopedia is an excellent sourcebook. It will explain many subjects of which the student has limited knowledge. When one comes across an obscure point in the biblical text or in a commentary, he can turn to a Bible dictionary to fill in the background. Probably the best recent works are the *Interpreter's Dictionary of the Bible* (Abingdon, 1962; with a 1977 *Supplement*); *The New Bible Dictionary* (Eerdmans, 1962); and the *Wycliffe Bible Encyclopedia* (2 vols., Moody, 1975). All of these deal concisely and thoroughly with a wide variety of topics and issues. *Baker's Dictionary of Theology* (Baker, 1960) centers on theological topics and is an excellent tool. Also, there are several multivolume works which deal more comprehensively with biblical topics. *The Zondervan Pictorial Encyclopedia* (5 vols., Zondervan, 1975), was ten years in preparation, and contains the best of evangelical scholarship. A forthcoming work of the same ilk is *The Tyndale Home Bible Encyclopedia*, the first volume of which will be published in 1980. The series under the editorship of James Hastings contains the classic works (*Dictionary of the Bible*, Scribner's, 1963; *Dictionary of Christ and the Gospels*, etc.); also important are *The Interpreter's Dictionary of the Bible* (4 vols., Abingdon, 1962); and *The International Standard Bible Encyclopedia* (5 vols., Eerdmans, 1939).

(3) A handbook or introduction to the Bible explains the basic problems and issues in Bible study. It is difficult for many students to understand the cohesion of the Bible, or to solve problems encountered in studying it. Two of the best general works in this area are David and Patricia Alexander, eds., *Eerdman's Handbook to the Bible* (Eerdmans, 1973); and Norman L. Geisler

and William E. Nix, *A General Introduction to the Bible* (Moody, 1968). The former is more of a classical introduction, dealing with the problems of interpretation and discussing the books of the Bible in turn. The latter discusses inspiration, canonization, and the transmission of the Bible—three crucial areas for understanding the Bible.

There are also several excellent introductions to each testament. The best Old Testament introductions are Roland K. Harrison, *Introduction to the Old Testament* (Eerdmans, 1964³); and Gleason L. Archer, *A Survey of Old Testament Introduction* (Moody, 1976²). The best New Testament introductions are Donald Guthrie, *New Testament Introduction* (InterVarsity Press, 1971); and Paul Feine and Johannes Behn, *Introduction to the New Testament*, ed. Werner G. Kummel (Abingdon, 1966). The former represents the evangelical wing and the latter the conservative Continental position. Of slightly less stature but still worthwhile are works by Everett F. Harrison, *Introduction to the New Testament* (Eerdmans, 1971); and Merrill C. Tenney, *New Testament Survey* (Eerdmans, 1961). The latter deals more with content and background material than with introductory matters such as authorship and style.

(4) Bible atlases, archaeology books, and background works can help the student visualize the scenes in the Bible. There are many good atlases and discussions of the geography of biblical times. The best is probably Y. Aharoni and M. Avi-Yonah, *The Macmillian Bible Atlas* (Macmillian, 1968). One might also use Charles F. Pfeiffer, ed., *Baker's Bible Atlas* (Baker, 1961). One of the best archaeological works is J. Finegan, *Light from the Ancient Past* (Princeton, 1959²), though for some students a less technical work may be better, such as Kenneth A. Kitchen, *The Bible in Its World* (InterVarsity, 1977), the best evangelical intro-

duction to date; or M. F. Unger, *Archeology and the Old Testament* (Zondervan, 1954) and *Archeology and the New Testament* (Zondervan, 1962).

Background works can greatly help the reader to understand the cultural context of a passage. The classic Old Testament work is probably Roland de Vaux, *Ancient Israel* (2 vols., McGraw-Hill, 1961); though some would prefer a more conservative work such as Kenneth A. Kitchen, *Ancient Orient and the Old Testament* (InterVarsity, 1966); F. F. Bruce, *Israel and the Nations* (Eerdmans, 1963); or Donald J. Wiseman, ed., *Peoples of the Old Testament* (Clarendon Press, 1973[4]). New Testament background works are multitudinous. General reference works are F. F. Bruce, *New Testament History* (Nelson, 1969); Bo Reicke, *The New Testament Era, The World of the Bible from 500 B.C. to A.D. 100*, (Fortress, 1968); Merrill C. Tenney, *New Testament Times* (Eerdmans, 1965); and F. V. Filson, *A New Testament History* (SCM, 1965). The standard work on Judaism is Emil Schürer, *A History of the Jewish People in the Time of Jesus Christ* (5 vols., Edinburgh: T & T Clark, 1890–91), now being revised and updated under the editorship of Gaza Vermes and Fergus Miller (T & T Clark, 1973). This work covers the period from 175 B.C. to A.D. 135. Less technical works are Charles F. Pfeiffer, *Between the Testaments* (Baker, 1959); Joachim Jeremias, *Jerusalem in the Time of Jesus* (Fortress, 1967); and the aforementioned *Israel and the Nations* by Bruce.

(5) Theological works help the student place everything in perspective. It is difficult to know where to begin in this field, for there is an enormous amount of literature available. Any time one labels a work "the best," he is labeling his own biases and theological preferences. Nevertheless, we will mention a few good works. From the Calvinist perspective, one might note Charles Hodge, *Systematic Theology* (3 vols., Nelson, 1872), L.

Berkhof, *Systematic Theology* (Eerdmans, 1946), or G. C. Berkouwer, *Studies in Dogmatics* (12 vols., Eerdmans, 1952). From the dispensational view is L. S. Chafer, *Systematic Theology* (8 vols., Zondervan, 1947). From the Arminian stance is W. B. Pope, *A Compendium of Christian Theology* (Wesley Conference Office, 1879); or H. C. Thiessen, *Introductory Lectures in Systematic Theology* (Eerdmans, 1949). These represent only a small portion of the works available, but they are a starting point for the student. Church libraries would also do well to purchase works in the other areas of theology, such as historical or contemporary theology, as well as the specific areas of bibliology, christology, and so forth.

Biblical theology is an extremely important field, and the student should note some of the significant works. Biblical theology serves as a balance between exegesis, with its narrow scope regarding individual passages, and systematic theology, with its broad scope regarding doctrinal trends. The classic evangelical work dealing with both testaments is Geerhardus Vos, *Biblical Theology* (Eerdmans, 1948). In Old Testament theology, evangelicals have not matched the scholarly depth and comprehensive coverage of the theologies by Eichrodt, Jacob, or Von Rad. Some of the best works are Walter Kaiser, *Towards an Old Testament Theology* (Zondervan, 1978), the best to date; J. Barton Payne, *Theology of the Older Testament* (Zondervan, 1962); and Edward J. Young, *The Study of Old Testament Theology Today* (Revell, 1959). A simpler, concise, yet still excellent work is H. L. Ellison, *The Message of the Old Testament* (Eerdmans, 1969). There are several good New Testament theologies. The best non-evangelical works are by Joachim Jeremias, Alan Richardson, and Ethelbert Stauffer. The best evangelical work is by George E. Ladd, *A Theology of the New Testament* (Eerdmans, 1974); with simpler works by Charles C. Ryrie, *Biblical Theology of the New Testament*

(Moody, 1959); and Chester K. Lehman, *Biblical Theology: New Testament* (Herald Press, 1974; a companion volume to Lehman's Old Testament theology).

(6) Books on Bible study methods explain how to better approach Scripture. There are, of course, many aspects to Bible study, and it is impossible to deal with all in one work (though it is hoped that this book will help fill in the gaps). A work describing the various methods (e.g., the inductive, synthetic, analytical, etc.) is Howard Vos, *Effective Bible Study* (Zondervan, 1956).[3] A good compendium discussing topics involved in Bible study (e.g., analyzing a book or passage, word study, etc.) is John B. Job, ed., *Studying God's Word* (InverVarsity Press, 1972).[4] A more comprehensive work, combining hermeneutics and Bible study methods is Robert A. Traina, *Methodical Bible Study: A New Approach to Hermeneutics* (Wilmore, Ky.: by the author, 1966).

(7) Books on hermeneutics will help the student avoid erroneous approaches to passages. One of the most difficult problems in Bible study is that each type of biblical material must be approached differently: poetry, prophecy, parables, commands, and so forth differ from each other in style and linguistic character and so must be interpreted as separate types of literature. A good general discussion is found in *Baker's Dictionary of Practical Theology* (Baker, 1967); the section in it on hermeneutics has been published separately as Bernard L. Ramm, et al., *Hermeneutics* (Baker, 1971). Two more complete works are Bernard L. Ramm, *Protestant Biblical Interpretation* (Baker, 1970); and A. Berkeley Mickelsen, *Interpreting the Bible* (Eerdmans, 1963).

(8) Greek study aids are indispensable for any student working with biblical Greek. This is mentioned last only because many readers are not familiar with Greek. Personally, we recommend that the pastor teach those in his congregation who are interested. If he does so, there are certain dangers to avoid: (a) An elitist

atmosphere in which those who know Greek consider themselves "more spiritual" than those who do not. This can be alleviated by stressing that Greek is no more than a study aid and elevates no one in God's eyes. (b) A tendency for the pastor to become too technical in sermons, so that he confuses those who do not know Greek. This is solved when the pastor constantly keeps in mind those who are unfamiliar with the language as he prepares sermons. (c) A general fear on the part of the majority at the very mention of Greek. This is the feeling of nearly every seminary student, so how can one expect any different from a congregation? The pastor must be very careful to show the congregation that Greek is not something to cause terror but a positive aid for understanding Scripture. This can be accomplished by the pastor's demeanor and approach (see conclusion).

Which beginning grammars are most helpful will depend on personal taste. The classic work is by J. Gresham Machen, *New Testament Greek for Beginners* (Macmillian, 1923), but it is outdated due to recent discoveries. A good later work is J. W. Wenham, *The Elements of New Testament Greek* (Cambridge, 1965). The major lexicon is W. F. Arndt and F. W. Gingrich, *A Greek-English Lexicon of the New Testament and Other Early Christian Literature* (University of Chicago Press, 1957). This lexicon has replaced Thayer's *Greek-English Lexicon* because Arndt and Gingrich have used the papyri and other discoveries. The classical grammar is F. Blass and A. Debrunner, *A Greek Grammar of the New Testament and Other Early Christian Literature*, trans. and ed. by R. W. Funk (University of Chicago Press, 1961). A less technical and in some ways more usable work is C. F. D. Moule, *An Idiom Book of New Testament Greek* (Cambridge, 1959²). A student with knowledge of Greek can utilize what has been called the major achievement of New Testament scholarship in this century, G. Kittel and G. Friedrich, eds., *Theological Dictionary of the New Testament* (10 vols.,

Eerdmans, 1964–1976). An excellent work which updates Kittel in some areas is Colin Brown, ed., *Dictionary of the New Testament* (3 vols., Zondervan, 1975–1978). This dictionary works from English terms and so is accessible to the non-Greek student.

Hebrew is also important. It is neglected compared to Greek but will do much the same for the student in the Old Testament that Greek will do for the student in the New. Perhaps the best beginning grammar is J. Weingreen, *A Practical Grammar for Classical Hebrew* (Clarendon Press, 1939). A more recent work is Thomas O. Lambdin, *Introduction to Biblical Hebrew* (Scribner's, 1971), but the book's organization is controversial. The major lexicon is P. Brown, S. R. Driver, and C. A. Briggs, *A Hebrew and English Lexicon of the Old Testament* (Clarendon Press, 1959); and the classic grammar is E. Kautzsh and A. E. Cowley, *Gesenius' Hebrew Grammar* (Clarendon Press, 1910). A simpler grammar is R. J. Williams, *Hebrew Syntax: An Outline* (University of Toronto Press, 1967). The Old Testament counterpart to Kittel is G. Johannes Botterweck and Helmer Ringgren, eds., *Theological Dictionary of the Old Testament* (Eerdmans, 1974–). This is more philological and less theological than Kittel, which makes it more laudatory to scholars but less useful for students of the Bible. A forthcoming work along this same line by evangelicals will be *A Theological Word Book of the Old Testament*, edited by G. Archer, R. L. Harris, and B. Waltke (Moody.)

Commentaries

There are several good sets of commentaries, although it may be wiser to select the best commentary for each biblical book rather than purchase an entire set. The advantage of a set (if by a single author) is a homogeneity of style and interpretation. The disadvantage (especially if there are many authors) is the diverse quality of the individual works within it. Nevertheless, some are well worth purchasing as sets, especially at a discount price.

(1) *One-volume commentaries.* The best single-volume works are M. Black and H. H. Rowley, *Peake's Commentary on the Bible* (Nelson, 1962); D. Guthrie, et al., *The New Bible Commentary: Revised* (Eerdmans, 1970); and C. F. Pfeiffer and E. F. Harrison, eds., *The Wycliffe Bible Commentary* (Moody, 1962). All three are excellent works and surprisingly exegetical. Peake's may be slightly more useful because of its greater comprehensiveness, especially in the topical articles, although it is not conservative. Another excellent work, written from a Roman Catholic perspective, is R. E. Brown, et al., *The Jerome Bible Commentary* (Prentice-Hall, 1968).

(2) *Multivolume sets.* There are several older sets on the entire Bible, the best of which is J. P. Lange, ed., *Commentary on the Holy Scriptures* (Zondervan, n.d.). A shorter work is R. Jamieson, A. R. Fausset, and D. Brown, *A Commentary Critical, Experimental and Practical on the Old and New Testaments* (6 vols., Eerdmans, 1948). However, these have not had access to newer discoveries in archeology, philology, and so forth, and it may well be better so select a more recent set, such as *The Tyndale Old* (and *New*) *Testament Commentaries* (Tyndale or InterVarsity Press) or *The New International Commentary* (Eerdmans). Individual commentaries from these sets will be mentioned below.

Commentary sets on the testaments are also helpful. A must for any student of the Old Testament is C. F. Keil and F. Delitzsch, *Biblical Commentary on the Old Testament* (Eerdmans, 1950). Although produced in the late nineteenth century, it is still unsurpassed for general exegetical excellence. And while it is based on the Hebrew, the experienced Bible student will have no trouble using it. The best New Testament sets are non-evangelical, such as the German Meyer series and the British Black series. There are also several good evangelical sets on the New Testament, such as William Hendriksen, *New Testament Commentary* (Baker). For those who know Greek, the best is probably W. R. Nicoll, ed., *The Expositor's Greek Testament* (Eerdmans, 1961); another good, though verbose, set is R. C. H. Lenski's series (Augsburg, 1943). Two forthcoming evangelical sets will be The New International Greek Testament series and the Word Commentary series. Both will maintain exceptional quality.

(3) *Individual commentaries.* The suggestions in this section will be given from the perspective of the general Bible student.

Genesis. The most insightful commentary here is H. C. Leupold, *Exposition of Genesis* (2 vols., Baker, 1942). Like Keil and Delitzsch, Leupold uses Hebrew, but in such a way that the untrained student can still gain much from it. A shorter, less comprehensive work is Derek Kidner, *Genesis: An Introduction and Commentary* (Tyndale series; Tyndale, 1967). Due to its brevity, important discussions are omitted, but it is still a valuable work. The more advanced student may wish to obtain Harold G. Stigers, *A Commentary on Genesis* (Zondervan, 1976), which provides good up-to-date archaeological data. A simpler discussion of background material is found in John J. Davis, *Paradise to Prison: Studies in Genesis* (Baker, 1975).

Exodus. There are several good works from which to choose. A good, concise work is R. Alan Cole, *Exodus: An Introduction and Commentary* (Tyndale series; InterVarsity, 1973). Another is John J. Davis, *Moses and the Gods of Egypt* (Baker, 1971), which is limited on critical issues but strong on background discussion. For the more advanced student, two excellent works are Umberto Cassuto, *A Commentary on the Book of Exodus* (Magnus Press, 1967); and Brevard S. Childs, *The Book of Exodus: A Critical Theological Commentary* (Westminster, 1974). The first is strong on exegetical data and the second on biblical theology, though the author is non-evangelical.

Leviticus. This is one of the neglected areas, and it is difficult to find much. Two of the best would be Samuel H. Kellogg, *The Book of Leviticus* (George H. Doran and Co., n.d.) and Andrew A. Bonar, *A Commentary on the Book of Leviticus* (Baker, 1978 reprint). Unfortunately, many of the evangelical works in this area contain little more than an overzealous use of typology, which rarely interprets the text.

Numbers. The Book of Numbers is even more neglected than the Book of Leviticus. We might mention H. D. M. Spence in *The Pulpit Commentary* (Eerdmans, 1950), and George Bush, *Notes, Critical and Practical on the Book of Numbers* (Irison & Phinney, 1858). J. H. Greenstone, *The Holy Scripture with Commentary: Numbers* (Jewish Publication Society, 1939), is a good, conservative Jewish study, though it is not equal in quality to Cassuto's scholarship.

Deuteronomy. An excellent exegetical study is Peter C. Craigie, *The Book of Deuteronomy* (New International; Eerdmans, 1976); another good commentary is John A. Thompson, *Deuteronomy: An Introduction and Commentary* (Tyndale series; InterVarsity, 1974). A good background study is Meredith G. Kline, *Treaty of the Great King* (Eerdmans, 1963).

Joshua. There are few good commentaries on the Book of Joshua. One good introduction is John J. Davis, *Conquest and Crisis: Studies in Joshua, Judges and Ruth* (Baker, 1969). Bush and Spence (see on Numbers) also have commentaries on Joshua. A book discussing Joshua but with little exegesis is Francis A. Schaeffer, *Joshua and the Flow of Biblical History* (InterVarsity, 1975).

Judges. A good, concise work is A. E. Cundall and L. Morris, *Judges and Ruth* (Tyndale series; Tyndale, 1968). Another is Leon Wood, *Distressing Days of the Judges* (Zondervan, 1975).

An excellent background work from a modern critical perspective is Andrew D. H. Mayes, *Israel in the Period of the Judges* (SCM, 1974).

Ruth. Several of the better works on the Book of Ruth have already been mentioned. A brief theological study is Ronald M. Hals, *The Theology of the Book of Ruth* (Fortress, 1969). Another short study is George A. Knight, *Ruth and Jonah: The Gospel in the Old Testament* (SCM, 1966).

I and II Samuel. A helpful approach to the historical books is W. D. Crockett, *A Harmony of the Books of Samuel, Kings and Chronicles* (Baker, 1951, reprint). A good introductory study is John J. Davis, *The Birth of a Kingdom: Studies in I and II Samuel and I Kings 1–11* (Baker, 1970). The more advanced student may wish to work through H. W. Hertzburg, *I and II Samuel: A Commentary* (Westminster, 1964); and one of the best non-evangelical studies of II Samuel is R. A. Carlson, *David: The Chosen King* (Almquist and Wiksells, 1964).

I and II Kings. There is not a great deal on these books apart from the Crockett and Davis series mentioned above. A non-evangelical work must be labeled the best here, though it is mainly for the more advanced student: John Gray, *I and II Kings: A Commentary* (Westminster, 1963). An evangelical study is John C. Whitcomb, *Solomon to the Exile: Studies in Kings and Chronicles* (Baker, 1971), though one could wish for a better interaction with the issues.

I and II Chronicles. In addition to the works already mentioned, we might note William Kelly, *Lectures on the Books of Chronicles* (Wilson Foundation, 1963), which is not very deep but is helpful in places.

Ezra and **Nehemiah.** Here again there has been very little quality work done by evangelicals. One good work is H. E. Ryle, *The Books of Ezra and Nehemiah* (Cambridge, 1917); another is by George Rawlinson in the Pulpit Commentary series.

Esther. One must once again go to the commentary series mentioned previously for good works on Esther. One exception is George A. F. Knight, *Esther, Song of Songs, Lamentations* (SCM, 1965), which is in places theologically uncertain, but a good study on the whole.

Job. A good study here is Frances I. Anderson, *Job: An Introduction and Commentary* (Tyndale series; InterVarsity, 1976). A good background study from a modern critical standpoint is the Jewish scholar Robert Gordis, *The Book of God and Man: A Study of Job* (University of Chicago, 1965). A shorter but good study is H. L. Ellison, *From Tragedy to Triumph: The Message of the Book of Job* (Eerdmans, 1958).

Psalms. There are many good conservative studies of the Psalms. The best are probably H. C. Leupold, *Exposition of the Psalms* Baker, 1969 reprint); J. J. S. Perowne, *The Book of Psalms* (Zondervan, 1966, reprint); and Derek Kidner, *Psalms: An Introduction and Commentary* (Tyndale series; 2 vols., InterVarsity, 1973–75).

Proverbs. The best evangelical work is Derek Kidner, *The Proverbs: An Introduction and Commentary* (Tyndale series; InterVaristy, 1964). More technical works are C. H. Toy, *A Critical and Exegetical Commentary on the Book of Proverbs* (International Critical Commentary; T & T Clark, 1959 reprint); and William McKane, *Proverbs: A New Approach* (Westminster, 1970). Neither is written from the conservative position, but the latter is an especially detailed discussion of the exegetical data.

Ecclesiates. The best evangelical work here is H. C. Leupold, *Exposition of Ecclesiastes* (Baker, 1966 reprint). Another good work is Derek Kidner (see on Proverbs). Two technical studies, written from the modern critical standpoint but with good exegetical discussion, are Robert Gordis, *Koheleth: The Man and His World* (Bloch, 1955); and the Jewish scholar Christian D. Ginsburg, *The Song of Songs and Koheleth* (Ktar, 1970).

Song of Solomon. Here also one is almost forced to turn to the single-volume commentaries and the older sets. Unfortunately, most of the evangelical works depart into a spiritualized application, and do not discuss the text. A recent work is *A Song for Lovers* by S. Craig Glickman (InterVarsity Press, 1976); but is a practical application rather than an expositional study. A modern Jewish study for the technical student is Ginsburg (see on Ecclesiastes).

Isaiah. The best evangelical study is Edward J. Young, *The Book of Isaiah* (3 vols., Eerdmans, 1965). The classic work is J. A. Alexander, *Commentary on the Prophecies of Isaiah* (Zondervan, 1953, reprint).

Jeremiah and **Lamentations.** One of the best works is R. K. Harrison, *Jeremiah and Lamentations: Introduction and Commentary* (Tyndale Series; InterVarsity, 1973). One with good sermonic helps is Theodore Laetsch, *Jeremiah* (Concordia, 1952). A classic work is C. Von Orellio, *The Prophecies of Jeremiah* (T & T Clark, 1889).

Ezekiel. The best work for the nonprofessional Bible student is probably John B. Taylor, *Ezekiel: An Introduction and Commentary* (Tyndale series; InterVarsity, 1969). Two others worth mentioning are H. L. Ellison, *Ezekiel: The Man and His Message* (Eerdmans, 1956), a good introductory discussion; and C. L. Feinberg, *The Prophecy of Ezekiel* (Moody, 1969), which takes a dispensational approach. For the technician, the classic work is G. A. Cooke, *A Critical and Exegetical Commentary on the Book of Ezekiel* (T & T Clark, 1936).

Daniel. There are a great number of good commentaries on Daniel. Three are worthy of equal mention: Edward J. Young, *The Prophecy of Daniel: A Commentary* (Eerdmans, 1949); H. C. Leupold, *Exposition of Daniel* (Baker, 1949, reprint); and Leon J. Wood, *A Commentary on Daniel* (Zondervan, 1973). The first two represent the amillennial, the third the premillennial perspective. An excellent exegetical study for the scholar is James A. Montgomery, *A Critical and Exegetical Commentary on the Book of Daniel* (T & T Clark, 1927).

Hosea. There are not many good evangelical treatments of Hosea. The best may be by Theodore Laetsch, *The Minor Prophets* (Concordia, 1956); and Edward Pusey, *The Minor Prophets: A Commentary, Explanatory and Practical* (2 vols., Baker, 1961, reprint). A popular treatment, more practical than exegetical, is David A. Hubbard, *With Bonds of Love* (Eerdmans, 1967). The best work available is by the modern critical scholar Hans Walter Wolff, *Hosea* (Fortress, 1974).

Joel. Here again one must turn to the single-volume and multivolume sets mentioned earlier, together with the volumes by E. B. Pusey and Theodore Laetsch (see on Hosea).

Amos. There are several quality commentaries on Amos. The best may well be J. A. Motyer, *The Day of the Lion: The Message of Amos* (InterVarsity, 1974), an excellent blend of exegetical and practical exposition. A good shorter discussion, but without the exegetical acumen of Motyer, is J. K. Howard, *Amos Among the Prophets* (Baker, 1968). A good technical work is R. A. Cripps, *A Critical and Exegetical Commentary on the Book of Amos* (Macmillian, 1955²).

Obadiah. The best work by far on Obadiah is L. C. Allen, *The Books of Joel, Obadiah, Jonah and Micah* (New International Series, Eerdmans, 1976). Allen uses the tools of the latest scholarship to provide some interesting exegetical suggestions. One might also mention John P. Watts, *Obadiah: A Critical Exegetical Commentary* (Eerdmans, 1969). Other than these, the sets are the best sources for material.

Jonah. Perhaps the best work again is Allen (see on Obadiah; see also the works by Pusey and Laetsch discussed under Hosea and the study by Knight mentioned under Ruth). Good expository discussion can be found in Patrick Fairbairn's classical study, *Jonah: His Life, Character and Mission* (Kregel, 1964 reprint).

Micah. See Allen, under Obadiah, for one of the best on this book (note also Pusey and Laetsch).

Nahum. The best work on this book, though perhaps too technical for many, is Walter A. Maier, *The Book of Nahum: A Commentary* (Concordia, 1959). Other than that, the commentary sets already mentioned are the best sources.

Habakkuk. An excellent study from the modern critical viewpoint is Donald E. Gowan, *The Triumph of Faith in Habakkuk* (John Knox, 1976), for it combines exposition and practical and homiletical data which helps to illuminate the book. Another book worth mentioning is John H. Eaton, *Obadiah, Nahum, Habakkuk and Zephaniah* (SCM, 1961), with many insightful comments. For sermonic minds, see D. Martyn Lloyd-Jones, *From Fear to Faith* (InterVarsity, 1953).

Zephaniah. Again, the commentary sets are the real sources of good material. We might mention here Hobart E. Freeman, *Nahum, Zephaniah, Habakkuk* (Moody, 1973). A good modern critical study is found in Arvid S. Kapelrud, *The Message of the Prophet Zephaniah* (Oslo: Universitets Forlaget, 1975).

Haggai. An excellent study is found in Joyce G. Baldwin, *Haggai, Zechariah, Malachi: An Introduction and Commentary* (Tyndale series; InterVarsity, 1972), which provides sound exegesis in a concise, simple style. Less valuable but still worthwhile for the average student is Richard Wolff, *The Book of Haggai* (Baker, 1967).

Zechariah. Here also we note several good works. Baldwin (see under Haggai) is probably the best, slightly better than H. C. Leupold, *Exposition of Zechariah* (Baker, 1971 reprint). We might also mention Merrill F. Unger, *Zechariah: Prophet of Messiah's Glory* (Zondervan, 1963).

Malachi. Again, Baldwin (see above) is a must. Apart from this, one should check the commentary sets.

Matthew. This Gospel has the least good commentaries of the four, though forthcoming works by Robert H. Gundry, Robert Guelich, and Herman Ridderbos should help to change the situation. For the average student, R. V. G. Tasker, *The Gospel of St. Matthew* (Tyndale series; Eerdmans, 1961), may be worthwhile, but it is probably too limited to satisfy. Floyd V. Filson, *A Commentary on the Gospel According to St. Matthew* (Black series; Harper & Row, 1960), contains much better coverage; and William Hendriksen, *New Testament Commentary: Matthew* (Baker, 1973) has a good discussion.

Mark. The best work here is William L. Lane, *The Gospel According to St. Mark* (New International series; Eerdmans, 1974), one of the best in this series, though it may be too difficult for some. An as good but simpler work is D. Edmond Hiebert, *Mark: A Portrait of the Servant* (Moody, 1974). The classic conservative work is by H. B. Swete, *The Gospel According to Mark* (Eerdmans, 1956 reprint).

Luke. The best work, though too technical for the average student, will be I. H. Marshall, *commentary on the Greek Text of Luke* (2 vols., Eerdmans, 1978). Another good work, which by and large follows Alfred Plummer, *A Critical and Exegetical Commentary on the Gospel According to St. Luke* (ICC: T & T Clark, 1896), is J. N. Geldenhuys, *Commentary on the Gospel of Luke* (New International series; Eerdmans, 1952). Perhaps the best for the less advanced student is Leon Morris, *The Gospel According to St. Luke* (Tyndale series; Eerdmans, 1974). With excellent exegetical data, it is far and away the best of the Tyndale studies on the Gospels and Acts.

John. The Book of John has more high quality treatments than any other book of the Bible. The best evangelical work on this book is by Leon Morris, *The Gospel According to John* (New International series; Eerdmans, 1971), a good study work and sermonic guide. The classical work, still worthwhile, is Brooke F. Westcott, *The Gospel According to St. John, Greek Text* (Eerdmans, 1955 reprint). For the less advanced, a good discussion is Merrill F. Tenney, *John: The Gospel of Belief* (Eerdmans, 1948). The advanced student should utilize the excellent works by C. K. Barrett, R. E. Brown, and R. Schnackenberg.

Acts. The best commentary on Acts must still remain F. F. Bruce, *The Acts of the Apostles* (New International series; Eerdmans, 1954), which is excellent in every way (see also his commentary on the Greek text, Eerdmans, 1952²). Three more recent works are also worthy of mention: William Neil, *The Acts of the Apostles* (New Century series: Attic Press, 1973), a good scholarly treatment; and two more popular studies: Everett F. Harrison's *Acts: The Expanding Church* (Moody, 1975), with excellent discussion of selected points; and William S. LaSor, *Church Alive* (Regal, 1972), probably the best of the Laymen's Bible Commentary series.

Romans. The best work here is C. E. B. Cranfield, *A Critical and Exegetical Commentary on the Epistle to the Romans* (ICC new series; T & T Clark, 1977). A less technical and more theological study is John Murray, *The Epistle to the Romans* (2 vols., New International series, 1959–1965). A good book for the average student is F. F. Bruce, *The Epistle of Paul to the Romans* (Tyndale series; Eerdmans, 1963), which is a little too brief but has many insightful comments. The classic work remains W. Sanday and A. C. Headlam, *A Critical and Exegetical Commentary on the Epistle to the romans* (ICC; Scribner's, 1897).

I Corinthians. The best commentary is probably C. K. Barrett, *A Commentary on the First Epistle to the Corinthians* (Black series; Harper & Row, 1968), a marvelous blend of exegetical insight and practical helps. Another good work is F. W.

Grosheide, *Commentary on the First Epistle to the Corinthians* (New International series; Eerdmans, 1953). Simpler yet worthwhile works are F. F. Bruce, *I and II Corinthians* (New Century series; Attic Press, 1971); Leon Morris, *The First Epistle of Paul to the Corinthians* (Tyndale series; Eerdmans, 1958); and Fred Fisher, *Commentary on I and II Corinthians* (Word, 1975). See also Héring, below.

II Corinthians. Again, the best commentary is by C. K. Barrett, *A Commentary on the Second Epistle to the Corinthians* (Black series; Harper & Row, 1976). Other good works are Phillip E. Hughes, *Paul's Second Epistle to the Corinthians* (New International series; Eerdmans, 1961); and Jean Héring, *The Second Epistle of Paul to the Corinthians* (Epworth, 1967). See also the works by Bruce and Fisher above.

Galatians. There are several good works on the Book of Galatians. The classical and probably still the best work is the ICC volume by E. D. Burton, *A Critical and Exegetical Commentary on the Epistle to the Galatians* (T & T Clark, 1920). Another is J. B. Lightfoot, *St. Paul's Epistle to the Galatians* (Zondervan, 1957, reprint). A less technical yet still excellent study is Donald Guthrie, *Galatians* (New Century series; Attic Press, 1969). Less valuable but still worthwhile for the nonprofessional are Alan Cole, *The Epistle of Paul to the Galatians* (Tyndale series; Eerdmans, 1965); and H. D. McDonald, *Freedom in Faith: A Commentary on Paul's Epistle to the Galatians* (Revell, 1973). A marvelous exposition is John R. W. Stott, *The Message of Galatians* (InterVarsity, 1968).

Ephesians. The best commentary, and one of the best on any New Testament book, is Markus Barth, *Ephesians* (2 vols., Anchor Bible series; Doubleday, 1974), although it is probably too technical for any but the advanced student. The classic works are by J. A. Robinson, *St. Paul's Epistle to the Ephesians* (Macmil-

lian, 1928²), which was until Barth the best work available; and
B. F. Westcott, *St. Paul's Epistle to the Ephesians* (Eerdmans,
1960, reprint). A simpler study is found in Francis Foulkes, *The
Epistle of Paul to the Ephesians* (Tyndale series; Eerdmans,
1963). William Hendriksen, *New Testament Commentary:
Ephesians* (Baker, 1967) has good sermonic material.

Philippians. Perhaps the best of the many good commentaries
on Philippians is J. B. Lightfoot, *St. Paul's Epistle to the Philippians* (Zondervan, 1953 reprint). Due to its technical nature,
however, the student may prefer Ralph P. Martin, *The Epistle of
Paul to the Philippians* (Tyndale series; Eerdmans, 1959), or his
update in the New Century series (Attic Press, 1977). One not
quite so conservative is F. W. Beare, *A Commentary on the
Epistle to the Philippians* (Black series; Harper & Row, 1959).
Finally, we might note Jacobus J. Müller, *The Epistles of Paul to
the Philippians and to Philemon* (New International series;
Eerdmans, 1955).

Colossians and **Philemon.** Excellent works here are Ralph P.
Martin, *Colossians and Philemon* (New Century series; Attic
Press, 1974); C. F. D. Moule, *The Epistles of Paul the Apostle to
the Colossians* (Cambridge, 1958); and J. B. Lightfoot, *Saint
Paul's Epistles to the Colossians and to Philemon* (Zondervan,
1959, reprint). The last is for the advanced student, but all con-
tain excellent exegetical interaction. Another good work is E. K.
Simpson and F. F. Bruce, *Commentary on the Epistles to the
Ephesians and Colossians* (New International series; Eerdmans,
1957). Simpson is notable for his prose, not for his exposition; but
Bruce, as usual, is excellent.

I and II Thessalonians. Perhaps the major work here, though
highly technical, is Ernest Best, *A Commentary on the Epistles to
the Thessalonians* (Black series; A & C Black, 1973). Only slightly
less valuable, however, and easier to use, is Leon Morris, *The
First and Second Epistles to the Thessalonians* (New International

series; Eerdmans, 1959). The classical works are by J. E. Frame, *A Critical and Exegetical Commentary on the Epistles of St. Paul to the Thessalonians* (ICC; T & T Clark, 1912); and G. Milligan, *St. Paul's Epistles to the Thessalonians* (Eerdmans, 1952, reprint). For the dispensational approach see D. Edmond Hiebert, *The Thessalonian Epistles* (Moody, 1971); for homiletical hints see William Hendriksen, *New Testament Commentary: I and II Thessalonians* (Baker, 1955).

The Pastoral Epistles. One of the finest commentaries in the New Testament field is J. N. D. Kelly, *A Commentary on the Pastoral Epistles: I Timothy, II Timothy, Titus* (Black series; Harper & Row, 1963), an excellent blend of background material and exegetical insights. Two shorter but still good works are Donald Guthrie, *The Pastoral Epistles: An Introduction and Commentary* (Tyndale series; Eerdmans, 1957), which is easier for the inexperienced student; and C. K. Barrett, *The Pastoral Epistles in the New English Bible with Introduction and Commentary* (Clarendon, 1963).

Hebrews. One can hardly do better than the gem by F. F. Bruce, *The Epistle to the Hebrews* (New International series; Eerdmans, 1964). However, one must note also the classic work by B. F. Westcott, *The Epistle to the Hebrews, The Greek Text* (Eerdmans, 1960, reprint) and the excellent theological study by Phillip E. Hughes, *A Commentary on the Epistle to the Hebrews* (Eerdmans, 1977). More for the average student is Thomas Hewitt, *The Epistle to the Hebrews: An Introduction and Commentary* (Tyndale series; Eerdmans, 1966). Two others worthy of mention are Jean Héring, *The Epistle to the Hebrews* (Epworth, 1970); and H. W. Montefiore, *A Commentary on the Epistle to the Hebrews* (Black series; Harper & Row, 1964).

James. A good study can be found in James Adamson, *The Epistle of James* (New International series, Eerdmans, 1976). Adamson interacts with the most recent theories and has several interesting suggestions. The classic work is J. B. Mayor, *The Epistle of St. James* (Zondervan, 1959, reprint); but an equally outstanding job was done by W. O. E. Oesterley in *The Expositor's Greek Testament*, ed. William R. Nicoll (5 vols., Eerdmans, 1951). Also worthy of mention are C. L. Mitton, *The Epistle of James* (Eerdmans, 1966); and R. V. G. Tasker, *The General Epistle of James* (Tyndale series; Eerdmans, 1957), a good choice for the average student.

I Peter. Two works deserve equal billing for excellence: J. N. D. Kelly, A *Commentary on the Epistles of Peter and Jude* (Black series; Harper & Row, 1969), which is nearly equal to his Pastoral Epistles commentary; and E. G. Selwyn, *The First Epistle of St. Peter* (Macmillian, 1947[2]), which will always be a classic but is too technical for the nonexpert. Three other excellent studies are Ernest Best, *I Peter* (New Century series; Attic Press, 1971); A. M. Stibbs, *The First Epistle General of Peter* (Tyndale series: Eerdmans, 1959), another good work for the layman; and F. W. Beare, *The First Epistle of Peter, The Greek Text* (Blackwell, 1969[3]).

II Peter and **Jude.** J. N. D. Kelly is again the best; however, close behind is E. M. B. Green, *The Second Epistle General of Peter and the General Epistle of Jude* (Tyndale series; Eerdmans, 1968). Other good works are J. B. Mayor, *The Epistle of St. Jude and the Second Epistle of St. Peter* (Baker, 1965 reprint); and C. A. Bigg, A *Critical and Exegetical Commentary on the Epistles of St. Peter and St. Jude* (ICC; T & T Clark, 1902[2]).

Johannine Epistles. There are many fine works on the Johannine Epistles. Two of these, often taught in seminaries as examples of the technical and expositional approaches (both are excellent), are B. F. Westcott, *The Epistles of St. John: The Greek Text with Notes* (Eerdmans, 1966 reprint); and J. R. W. Stott, *The Epistles of John* (Tyndale series; Eerdmans, 1964). An extremely valuable recent work is I. H. Marshall, *The Epistles of John* (New International series; Eerdmans, 1978). It is perhaps the best exegetical treatment to date. Other good studies are F. F. Bruce, *The Epistles of John* (Revell, 1970); Robert Law, *The Tests of Life: A Study of the First Epistle of St. John* (Baker, 1968 reprint); and C. H. Dodd, *The Johannine Epistles* (Hodder & Stoughton, 1946).

The Apocalypse. There are perhaps more commentaries on this enigmatic writing than any other single biblical book. There are several good studies, and what one considers best may well depend on one's eschatological presuppositions. For the amillennial position, there are several excellent ones: G. R. Beasley-Murray, *The Book of Revelation* (New Century series; Attic Press, 1974), perhaps the best; Leon Morris, *The Revelation of St. John* (Tyndale series; Eerdmans, 1969), a good work for the average student; G. B. Caird, *A Commentary on the Revelation of St. John the Divine* (Black series; Harper & Row, 1966), probably the most readable and a masterful work; and William Hendricksen, *More Than Conquerors* (Baker, 1939), one of Hendriksen's best works. For premillennial position, the best (perhaps even better than Beasley-Murray) is R. H. Mounce, *The Book of Revelation* (New International series; Eerdmans, 1977). Also see the good commentary by George E. Ladd, *A Commentary on the Revelation of John* (Eerdmans, 1972). The dispensational position is best represented by John F. Walvoord, *The Revelation of Jesus Christ* (Moody, 1966).

Conclusion

In selecting and using these works, one must carefully evaluate his or her own ability and interests. To select a work which is too difficult could lead to discouragement, disinterest, and eventually, apathy. It is important for the student to start with simpler works, like the Tyndale series (though even some of these are complex and technical for the beginner), then work his way up to the more difficult works. Bible study is an exciting new experience, especially as one discovers hidden truths in verses. It is hoped that this select list will enable each reader to progress in discovery and enlightenment as God's Word becomes more real and relevant in his or her life. If one's study time is used carefully and with prayer, it will become a precious flower, opening up exciting vistas of beauty as one carefully nourishes its meaning in his or her life.

This chapter has dealt with the "what" of Bible study—what tools to use, and what books to select for a well-rounded Bible study library. The next two chapters will attempt to instruct the reader regarding the "how" of Bible study. We will go on to detail principles of exegesis and apply them to general Bible study and sermonic preparation.

Notes

1. Two books to aid a church in developing a library program are Elmer L. Towns and Cyril J. Barber, *Successful Church Libraries* (Grand Rapids: Baker, 1971); and Gladys E. Scheer, *The Church Library: Tips and Tools* (St. Louis: Bethany Press, 1973). See the bibliographies in each for other works in this area.

2. Cyril J. Barber, *The Minister's Library: Periodic Supplement #1* (Grand Rapids: Baker, 1976). The basic text was published in 1974, and *Periodic Supplement #2* was released in 1978.

3. Vos relies on the classic work by Merrill C. Tenney, *Galatians: Charter of Christian Liberty* (mentioned in chap. 1, note 7).

4. Due to the nature of this compendium, some of the articles are less conservative than others.

6

Tools for Students

In previous chapters we noted the two basic aspects of Bible study—personal involvement with the text itself and the use of external tools such as commentaries. Most students tend to emphasize one over the other, which results in an imbalanced approach to the Word.

God's Word itself demands a balanced approach. As early as Joshua 1:8, which expands a theme repeated throughout Deuteronomy (4:40; 5:31–33; 17:19–20; etc.), we note the three-step process of true Bible study. We call this process the "three R's" of the Christian life—reading, reflecting, reacting.

The first part of the process is reading or memorizing the Word—a good translation of Joshua 1:8 might be, "You will never stop mentioning the book of the law," that is, you will go over and over it, and get to know it intimately.

The second part is reflecting or meditating on what you have learned—"You will meditate on it day and night." The word "meditate" translates the Hebrew word for "mutter," which pictures the rabbi constantly muttering to himself as he tried to understand the text. At that time written Hebrew contained only consonants; and so the rabbis, even though they had memorized the text, had to reflect continuously to arrive at the correct words (by adding the vowels) and discover a coherent text. In other words, it is not enough to know a passage if you do not understand what it means. For the rabbis, tradition developed and eventually took the form of commentaries, to help them bridge this gap. [1] The same is true of us; we dare not neglect either our own insights or the opinions of other scholars. The true student will seek not only the surface meaning but also an in-depth understanding of the text before he proceeds to discover its application to his life. The most important part of the message is the Word itself rather than the student's own thoughts.

Note that the third aspect of Bible study, reacting to the Word, that is, applying it to our lives, comes last. Too often we are guilty of reversing the order, determining a "spiritual truth" and then forcing the passage to fit. Only when we have allowed the Bible to speak for itself can we say we have interpreted it correctly. Therefore, we must above all learn how to do detailed exegesis and then how to apply the results of this study to the Christian life.

Attitudes for Doing Research

Before one can begin studying the Bible properly, he or she must develop the proper attitudes toward this endeavor. This can hardly be overemphasized, because one's attitude will determine how he or she will perform the task.

(1) *Love for truth.* The essential key to proper Bible study is a desire to know what God's Word actually says. This desire must be cultivated and worked at before it will come. Unfortunately, it can be argued that the average person has very little concern for truth. Most of us would prefer that "all things continue as they were" than admit we have been wrong. Truth is often very difficult and dangerous, and we have to fight ourselves as well as our opponents in order to arrive at it. It takes constant self-discipline

and effort to force ourselves to seek the true meaning of the text and then to do something about it.

(2) *Openness to other ideas.* Rudolf Bultmann wrote an influential article entitled, "Is Exegesis Without Presuppositions Possible?"[2] Most would agree with his conclusion that it is not possible. However, it is one thing to realize that one's presuppositions will influence the interpretation and another thing to follow blindly one's own *a priori* conclusions. A person who does the latter is seldom open to ideas which conflict with his own. A desire for truth means that each one must allow his presuppositions to be challenged and must be willing to change them if the evidence warrants. Needless to say, this is more easily said than done. As we mentioned in the introductory chapter, people would rather have their ideas confirmed than challenged. However, we must realize that we are greatly influenced by our environment, and much of our learning has been by chance rather than as a result of a deliberate search for truth. It is an exciting challenge to read the works of men who have grown up in different environments, and to interact with their unique ideas, integrating and changing as the evidence demands. There is an absolute, the Word of God, and a transient, man's interpretation. Our task is to study the latter so as to conform it to the former.

(3) *Critical but constructive approach.* Many students erroneously approach commentaries with the assumption that the writers are correct because they are "experts." But commentators' interpretations are also governed by presuppositions which may not be correct. Students must be able to examine the data critically as they use it in their study. At the same time, however, they must avoid the critical attitude which listens to a sermon or examines a book only in order to discover the errors. The student's task is to use the external material to supplement and modify his own conclusions. Therefore, he has a positive rather

than a negative purpose, and seeks insights which will aid a proper understanding of the passage's original meaning. Commentaries and other source material have a rich backlog of material to share with us; they will add valuable insight and data to our own knowledge.

(4) *Willingness to take time.* Few worthwhile things in life come easily. The old maxim, "You get what you pay for," is true in Bible study as well. It is also true that people are willing to spend a lot of time doing what they enjoy. Most Christians profess to care about the Bible yet are unwilling to spend a great deal of time studying it. We challenge readers to be willing to spend the same amount of time studying the Bible that they would spend playing tennis or golf. Church is the place where one takes lessons from the "expert" (the pastor) and in the quiet time one puts the points into practice. But this book will be almost useless unless each reader is willing to spend five to six hours a week digging into the Bible.

Research Methodology

Martin Luther had three rules for theological research: (1) *oratio*, the vertical aspect, involving prayer to God for guidance; (2) *meditatio*, the objective aspect, involving reading and contemplation of various views; and (3) *tentatio*, the subjective side, involving personal decision regarding the meaning of the text.[3] At all times we must recognize that it is the Holy Spirit, not ourselves or our source material, who leads us into truth. Yet the Spirit uses the tools of our own minds and our resource material in illuminating scriptural truth. The Spirit does not work in a vacuum, dictating to us the background and meaning of biblical texts. For this reason we must learn the proper procedure for exegeting a passage and must seek a correct blend of the subjective (the study of the text by itself) and objective (the use of external tools) factors. Here it would be helpful to cover steps already discussed in previous chapters from a slightly different perspective, that is, the use of other study aids.

(1) *Study the historical and logical context.* Knowledge of the circumstances which surrounded the writing of the book can be valuable for interpreting individual passages. In fact, the identification of the historical problems which led to the writing of the book is crucial to the exegetical task. With regard to the Minor Prophets, for instance, it is important to know when each was written in the history of its period. Otherwise, it would be easy to misunderstand some of the specific passages.

Also, the student should discover the major emphasis of the individual book. This is important, for example, in studying the Gospels. Each writer highlighted certain aspects of Christ's teaching and selected his stories accordingly. One of Luke's special interests is social justice. This realization is helpful in interpreting the difficult parables in 14:7–14 on the precedence at table and the excluded guests. While many have stressed the spiritual side of the parables, dealing with God's acceptance of the sinner, Luke shows that one's own attitude toward the poor is a determining factor in one's spiritual state. Verse 11 has often been taken as the conclusion to the first parable, but in actuality it is the connecting link between the two: "For everyone who exalts himself will be humbled, and he who humbles himself will be exalted." The self-seeking person who always aligns himself with the affluent and neglects the downtrodden will be judged harshly by God.

Knowing the cultural circumstances of the original readers can be of tremendous help, since the author would naturally write with a keen awareness of their perspective. In Philippians 4:7 Paul concludes the passage on prayer (vv. 6–7) with the phrase "and the peace of God . . . will guard your hearts and minds in Christ Jesus." The word for "guard" here is not the usual Greek word employed in the New Testament. It has the special idea of building a garrison or fort. The knowledge that Philippi was a Roman garrison town adds great meaning to the passage. Philippi was especially favored by this, because the presence of a Roman garrison brought a security which few towns felt. When the Gauls attacked from the north, they would raid Thessalonica or Berea, but never Philippi. To the Philippians, then, Paul was saying that God would produce a security and protective power in one's life which the arrows of worry could never pierce.

Finally, we should note the immediate context of the passage. Where does it fit in the developing argument of the book? This makes a great difference in the meaning of Philippians 3:13, "forgetting the things which are behind." On the face of it one would interpret the things forgotten as past failures and mistakes, dealing with the problem of guilt. However, the emphasis of 3:4–6 shows exactly the opposite. Paul is actually thinking of past gains, or successes. He claims they are meaningless, indeed, they are "dung" compared to the overriding privilege of knowing Christ.

This sort of context acknowledgment will be dealt with in greater detail under the section on hermeneutics later in the chapter, for misuse of Scripture is a major problem in evangelical circles today. "Proof-texting," that is, using a verse out of context to support a point without considering its actual contextual meaning, is a widespread practice. Christians must learn to interpret a verse in its original setting before they use it in argumentation.

There are several sources from which contextual information may be obtained: introductions to the better commentaries, works of introduction to the testaments, survey books, and general background works. The latter may be especially helpful on special topics, such as the sacrificial system or Roman law. Dictionaries and encyclopedias often have good discussions to help the student understand specific details.

(2) *Make a preliminary reading and outline of the passage.* This has already been dealt with in detail in chapter 3, but we must stress that the outline derived is tentative, because later research and exegesis will often lead the student to alter earlier decisions. In the preliminary outline the student will note the major emphasis of the passage and discover words or phrases for special study. By comparing several different commentaries one can see just how difficult outlining can be; often there are as many different outlines as there are commentaries. This does not mean the task is impossible, but it does mean there is no such thing as a "final outline." Thus the student will continue revising his outline as he goes along.

There are two major criteria for determining an outline of a passage: the grammatical organization of the sentences and the development of thought in the context. Often the thought development will take precedence over the grammatical organization, so one dare not depend on grammatical exegesis alone. This is especially true for Paul, since he often uses subordinate points as major digressions. An example would be Ephesians 1:3–14, which in the original Greek is one continuous, extremely complex sentence. A grammatical outline would be hopelessly detailed, but actually there are just two major points, the glory of God's elect will (vv. 3–10) and the union of Jew and Gentile in election (vv. 11–14). These then can be divided into subcategories: in the first instance, blessing the Godhead (v. 3), glory in election (vv. 4–6), glory in redemption (vv. 7–8), and glory in revelation (vv. 9–10); in the second instance, "we" chosen by God (vv. 11–12) and "you" sealed with the Holy Spirit (vv. 13–

14). The student must blend the two, basing his or her outline on the grammatical (cf. chap. three) but revising it if the thought development of the passage dictates.

Here also we might note the value of the biblical languages. While they are not absolutely essential for an understanding of the passage, they are a tremendous help in following the development of the author's ideas. It is one thing to know the general thrust of the "love" passage in John 21:15-17, but quite another thing to study the complicated interplay of synonyms in it. There are two words for "love," two for "know," two for "feed," and three for "sheep." In fact, the major stress is not on the "love" question but on the responsibility to "feed my flock," dealing with pastoral duty (cf. I Peter 5:1-4). While it is not absolutely necessary that every believer learn Greek and Hebrew, it is important that pastors know and use both in sermon preparation and in private study. It is our belief that any pulpit ministry would improve considerably if the languages were properly used.[4]

(3) *Exegete the passages phrase by phrase.* It is impossible to determine the detailed emphases of a passage after only superficial observation. Therefore, a detailed exegesis is crucial in deciding what to include and what to omit in the final lesson, sermon, or study. If Scripture is truly the Word of God, every nuance has eternal value; and it is the responsibility of every Christian to consider it carefully. The skimming method, where one skips over large portions and stops only at what he *believes* are the highlights, is inadequate by any standard. Yet this is the approach most of us take. Of course, it is also possible to over-exegete, that is, to draw out conclusions never really intended by the author. As we develop in experience and in understanding the first-century mind-set, this danger is minimized. We must keep asking, "What did the writer intend to say?" instead of asking, "What do I want this passage to say?"

As we have already stated, the student's first step is to go over the passage himself and note what he believes it is saying. Next, he supplements his study with commentaries and resource material. He carefully thinks through the comments made. After comparing them with his preliminary conclusions, he observes how they fit the historical and logical context of the passage.

The next step is to choose the major terms and concepts and do extra background study on those. For instance, what about the ceremony of the red heifer alluded to in Hebrews 9:13? One would want to look up the parallel passages, such as Numbers 19:2, and perhaps check with a good Bible dictionary to see what point the author is making. Hebrews is an exciting study when one takes the time to understand the Old Testament background. The student begins to feel the excitement of the early Jewish Christians and sees Christ in a new way as the fulfillment of the Old Testament expectation. The dynamic of the first-century church is recaptured by an in-depth exposure to this marvelous book.

(4) *Use the better commentaries.* In any study the researcher is limited in the number of books he can use. Therefore he must choose only the better works and restrict himself to these. It would be reckless to use a skimpy commentary on Acts when F. F. Bruce is available. The previous chapter attempted to discuss the better works in each area, and the student would be advised to use these. Some may seem dry and academic, but when the insights are added to one's own, they suddenly transform the passage and shed new light on its teaching. Often the more glamorous writers have less content to contribute; the student should never confuse rhetoric for depth. The true student seeks understanding rather than entertainment.[5]

(5) *Learn to use other resource material.* One of the best sources for material is periodical articles. The serious Bible stu-

dent who lives near a Bible college or seminary will want to use their resources. Indices such as *Christian Periodical Index, Index to Religious Periodical Literature, Religious and Theological Abstracts, Old Testament Abstracts,* and *New Testament Abstracts* catalogue articles by both passage and topic. One can look up a reference in the index and check any detailed articles (for instance, the note on the rabbis and Joshua 1:8 earlier in this chapter [p. 137] was found in a *Christianity Today* article). Also, the student would do well to subscribe to a few periodicals such as *Christianity Today, His* or *Journal of the Evangelical Theological Society* (for the more advanced student) and collate their articles with his own discoveries. The fact is that these articles often go into greater detail than the best commentaries and so contain valuable insights. We recommend a filing system which is organized according to topic and Scripture reference. It is not difficult to keep up to date and is itself a valuable study aid.

Also, the student should learn how to do word studies on important terms. The student who does not know the languages must be aware of certain problems: (1) Translations for a Greek or Hebrew word are seldom the same in every instance, so an English concordance can be misleading. The solution is to use Young's concordance or W. E. Vine, *An Expository Dictionary of New Testament Words* (Westwood, N.J.: Revell, 1940), which give the various Greek words (or Hebrew, in Young's concordance) behind an English word. The student then would trace through the Bible the specific word used in the text he is studying. (2) It is seldom adequate to trace a single word as the key to the biblical concept. The solution is to do a "theme study," noting synonyms and cognates which add nuances to the meaning of the term. The student must become acquainted with the whole of which the term used in the text is a part. Here one must take careful note of the place the particular verse has in relation to the broader context of the theme.

The process of word study, then, is not an easy one. The purist or scholar will wish to do original work, looking up the term and related concepts in the concordances and tracing the background in the Old Testament, cognate languages, intertestamental literature, and New Testament. The average student, however, will want to use the secondary helps, such as *Theological Dictionary of the New Testament* or *Theological Dictionary of the Old Testament* (in process of publication) or Brown's *Dictionary of New Testament Theology* for detailed, technical discussion. Or he may consult the other dictionaries, encyclopedias, and the like for less detailed coverage. In addition, those who have access to libraries can often find specialist works discussing a specific term. For example, soteriological terms such as "redemption," "covenant," "blood," and so on are analyzed with excellent perception in Leon Morris' *The Apostolic Preaching of the Cross* (Grand Rapids: Eerdmans, 1956). Finally, one dare not neglect the better commentaries; Brown on John, Cranfield on Romans, or Barth on Ephesians, to name just a few, will have good excurses on important terms.

The one warning to give the student who is depending on secondary sources, however, is to study the articles carefully and refuse to assume their accuracy. Like all human beings, scholars fall prey to their own biases and often treat contrary evidence with scant regard. It is wise to compare several opinions, think through the discussion, note the passages each scholar uses to support his conclusions, and check carefully to determine whether or not the data truly leads to his conclusions. As with exegesis proper, the scholars' insights must become the student's insights before he dares use it in his study. The student must also make certain he follows the hermeneutical rules before finalizing his word study.

(6) *Organize the data under a rearranged outline.* It is important that one realizes the necessity of categorizing and interpreting the data, checking it for reliability and formulating conclusions. Otherwise, one will end up with isolated and unrelated points, without order or relevance to the flow of thought in the passage. The danger of detailed Bible study like this can be illustrated by the many commentaries (even good ones) which isolate each word and discuss the terms one at a time. The result is that each word becomes separated from the others, an island of its own with little or no connection to the flow of narrative. The student never realizes the connection between the terms themselves.

The best approach would be to make the word studies the preliminary data and then discuss them under a rearranged outline. The data would lead the student to rework his original outline, and this in turn would help him to place the individual studies within the context of the developing passage. One difficulty in exegesis is the verse arrangement in our modern Bibles. It would be better for the student to discuss the passage on the basis of his outline and to use the verse division only to designate where he is in the passage. Thereby he would avoid such difficulties as Colossians 2:1–5, which belongs more with 1:24–29 than with 2:6f. Also, we avoid isolating "verses" from their context, as is the case when ministers preach Romans 8:28 but neglect its connection with 8:29–30.

(7) *State conclusions succinctly and with proper evidence.* Exegesis should at all times be fresh and original. The student should assimilate the data rather than woodenly summarizing other men's work. He must come to his own conclusions and must be selective, commenting only on data which provided

deeper insight into the author's message and into that aspect the student is stressing in his study. He should avoid extensive treatment of the peripheral and focus on intensive study of the key elements of the passage. The modern reader should try to catch the flavor of the passage itself as it would have been understood by the original readers.

The key to a relevant study lies not only in gathering evidence, but in presenting it properly. First, the facts must be verified. There are three aids to judgment: reports on a subject, observation and inference, and competent witness.[6] At the outset, one must clarify simple obscurities due to carelessness, bring the facts together, question small details, and seek the probable answers. One must learn to unravel facts, for the degree of success depends on one's grasp of the subject and the quality of the research. Second, hypotheses or conclusions must fit the verified facts. Above all, the evidence must be marshalled with the skeptic in mind, that is, it must be thoroughly and logically presented. A critic will deny one's conclusions if a single element is presented weakly.

The same should be true of sermons. The pastor should not be content merely to satisfy his congregation. He should teach them and lead them along the exciting road of self-discovery. Dialogue with the congregation on the points of the message is a useful and increasingly popular tool. For instance, a minister can show members of the congregation through dialogue how they *could* disagree with one of the points and think it through carefully. To many pastors this would be threatening, but it need not be. The dialogue will be constructive, not destructive, and will help members to become Bible students and not just listeners.

While most students will be exegeting passages for personal Bible study rather than for lesson presentation, this section on presentation is not invalid for them. Hopefully, they will return to the passage again and will need to build on their previous study. At that time a coherent and concise examination of the evidence will be important. They will want to rethink their conclusions and learn from past mistakes. A proper approach the first time is crucial to this future learning experience.

(8) *Apply the results of exegesis to daily life.* There has often been a false dichotomy between the meaning of the text and its practical implications for one's present needs.

Exegesis without application is not academic; exposition that is not grounded in exegesis is either superficial or misleading or even both. . . . Application is not a second and dispensable activity after exegesis, but in the normal situation exegesis leads inevitably to application.[7]

The Bible is never merely theory—it contains hard-core, dynamic, life-situational principles. It cannot be divorced from life without being destroyed. At the same time, however, it must be understood before being applied, lest a false lifestyle be introduced into the church. Therefore, the last step of exegesis (*not a separate step*) is the application of the conclusions to one's present situation: "How should *my* life be changed by what I've learned?" Here one must cross the gap between biblical principles and his own behavior, asking how the principles are meant to be applied.

This approach will seem idealistic or intimidating to many. Many people will consider it impractical and impossible time-wise. However, this is not true for the person willing to study for even five to six hours a week, which is less time than most people spend reading their newspaper or working on their lawn. Our desire is to challenge the reader to begin the adventure of Bible discovery.

Laws of Hermeneutics

Before one can properly do exegesis, one must learn hermeneutics, which refers to rules for interpretation. The history of the church confirms the necessity of such a code, for many erroneous movements have begun because of a mishandling of the Bible. Paul warns the Corinthians against a false approach which corrupts the Word of God (II Cor. 2:17), and commands Timothy to handle Scripture accurately (II Tim. 2:15). A proper hermeneutics is at the heart of true Bible study, yet few believers have any knowledge of the science. An arbitrary approach to interpretation occurs in far too many churches. We forget that communication is difficult enough when one is talking to a member of the same social and cultural circle (consider how many misunderstandings occur within families!), yet we are dealing here with material written centuries ago within a culture alien to our experience.

This cultural and linguistic gap can be bridged only when one has learned the rules for interpreting material from the other time and other culture. Of course, a detailed discussion of hermeneutical principles is impossible here, and we recommend the purchase of some of the works discussed in chapter 4. Here we will attempt a more general discussion aimed to help the student in basic Bible study. We cannot go into specific areas such as the interpretation of parables, apocalyptic, or psalms. That will be learned by studying the hermeneutical textbooks.

(1) *Trace the historical background of the passage or word.* The cultural gap is the major difficulty in interpretation, and one must uncover the cultural intention of the author before one can put it in the language of today. The key is to ask constantly, "Why did he say it this way?" and "What historical factors lie

behind its form?" As stated above in the section on exegesis, this data can best be found in background works and commentaries. The major hermeneutical rule here is the necessity of recreating the historical context behind the phrasing. The Germans call this the *Sitz im Leben* ("situation in life"), and an understanding of it will unlock many a mystery in the interpretation of a difficult text. This can be tremendously helpful in "synoptic" study (which analyzes the similarities and differences between the first three Gospels). For example, does Mark's reporting of the centurion's statement in Mark 15:29 ("Truly this man was the Son of God") contradict Luke's account in Luke 23:47 ("Certainly this man was innocent")? On the surface it seems so but the answer is to be found in the purpose of each author. Many scholars believe Luke was, in fact, *interpreting* Mark's "Son of God"; the similarities in vocabulary and tone indicate this, and the word "innocent," or "righteous" is actually the meaning of "Son of God" from the Roman perspective. [8] For Mark, it culminates his "Son of God" christology, while for Luke it concludes his stress on Jesus' innocence and righteous suffering. Therefore, each author focused on a different aspect of the same statement.

(2) *Interpret each biblical passage according to the literary laws of its genre.* It is wrong to treat a parable and a narrative in the same way, or prophetic passages like parenetic sections. Each type of literature must be approached differently. For example, one cannot build a doctrine of the afterlife on the interpretation of the parable of the rich man and Lazarus. The concept of a compartmentalized Hades occurs only there in Scripture, and we do not know that Christ meant this to be a precise eschatological instruction. Each parable is meant to teach a single point, and we are in danger if we take the details too far. The central message of the rich man and Lazarus is the danger of misusing wealth; we dare not build too much on the peripheral details. On the other

hand, each point of a parenetic section is important, and often the key to one aspect is found in a previous point. For example, the subjection of the wife in Ephesians 5:22f is not a chauvinistic command, for the love of the husband in verse 25 must also be subsumed under verse 21, "be subject one to another in the fear of Christ." Indeed, the verb "be subject" is not even found in verse 22, but is borrowed from verse 21. The wife's role is subjection to the leadership of her husband, but the husband's role as leader is one of self-sacrificial love. This means that the husband subjects his interests and desires to the needs of his wife. The result in the marital relationship is *mutual* subjection.

(3) *Recognize the priority of the original languages.* It is a common failing of Christians to treat versions as infallible translations. The classic (if apocryphal) assertion, "If the King James Version was good enough for the apostle Paul, it's good enough for me," is not far off the track in describing many Christians' attitudes toward the particular version they use. Too many times in our churches teachers have taken a particular word in the Living Bible paraphrase, for example, and built great doctrinal edifices upon it without regard for the fact that it may not even reflect the original passage. The Bible student can overcome this handicap by an educated use of the better commentaries. Above all, everyone must be aware of the dangers. The student should compare the translations as he studies the passage, and should take none of them for granted.

(4) *Recognize the analogical character of the Bible.* As God's revelation, the Bible must necessarily accommodate itself to the finite mind of man. The interpreter must beware of an overly literal interpretation of such phrases as "the hand of God," or "God changed his mind." Also, we cannot state with certainty that the streets of heaven are literally paved with gold or that eternal punishment will involve fire as we know it. We need to

recognize that much of Scripture is analogous because eternal realities are beyond our understanding.

At the same time, eternal truth was revealed progressively as God brought more and more truth to bear on His people. There is a danger in reading too developed a doctrine into earlier biblical passages. Recognizing this helps us to answer some ethical problems like polygamy among the patriarchs or the principle of jihad in the Old Testament. It should also help us to avoid the dangers of typology, such as reading New Testament theology back into Old Testament religious experience, of finding elaborate New Testament truths in every splinter of the tabernacle, and so forth.

(5) *Interpret according to the narrower context before the wider.* It is commonly agreed that Scripture should be used to interpret Scripture. However, it needs to be understood that a term or passage must be interpreted first in its immediate context before it is studied in light of its broader application to the Bible as whole. A frequent error is to interpret a phrase by Paul on the basis of its use in John. However, we must realize that each biblical writer, like each of us, used language differently. In fact, most of us use words differently than we did ten to fifteen years ago. This means that the student must be careful even when comparing Thessalonians to Ephesians, since they were written in two different periods in Paul's life.

It is crucial to interpret a phrase first by its use in its own immediate context, then by its use in the broader sphere of the major section of the work, then by its use in the book as a whole (check cross references). Next one may check the corpus of works by the same author. Only after that would one check the concept throughout the testament and then in the Bible as a whole. Each sphere has a progressively weaker influence on the meaning of the phrase, although all are important in the final analysis. For example, one would never wish to interpret Paul's concept of faith and works on the basis of James' discussion in 2:14–17, but at the same time it is significant that one show the relationship between them, that is, that Paul speaks of saving faith as separate from religious legal acts while James speaks of true Christian faith as inextricably bound up with the way one conducts his or her life. Faith cannot come via works, but it must result in works.

(6) *Look for the simplest interpretation.* Most people look for complex explanations. This is especially true of those who tend to allegorize Scripture, or make fanciful and imaginative reconstructions of simple biblical texts. However, these seldom reflect the actual meaning intended by the writer. And, while this approach may entertain and provoke the audience, its danger is that there are no controls to ensure that truth is being taught. Spiritualizing a text does not necessarily lead to spiritual truth.

Notes

1. Found in H. C. Leupold, *Christianity Today*, July 5, 1959.
2. Found in *Existence and Faith: Shorter Writing of Rudolf Bultmann*, ed. Schubert Ogden (New York: World Publishing Co., 1960).
3. Found in John W. Montgomery, "The Theologian's Craft," in *The Suicide of Christian Theology* (Minneapolis: Bethany Fellowship, 1970), p. 289.
4. Too few Greek or Hebrew teachers in college or seminary make the languages practical for the pulpit. The students must be shown how the language will enhance their study of Scripture.
5. We must, of course, note the importance of good rhetoric in teaching a passage. But that is the subject of the next chapter. Here we are discussing commentaries, not sermons.
6. Found in J. Barzun and H. F. Graft, *The Modern Researcher* (New York: Harcourt, Brace and World, 1970[2]), pp. 99f.
7. *Baker's Dictionary of Practical Theology*, ed. Ralph G. Turnbull (Grand Rapids: Baker, 1967), p. 101.
8. See Leon Morris, *The Gospel According to Luke* (Tyndale series; Grand Rapids: Eerdmans, 1974), p. 330.

7

Tools for Pastors and Teachers

A further application of the Bible study methods already discussed would be in the "professional" area of the pastor and teacher. Of course, in the Ephesians 4:11 sense,[1] pastors are by definition "teachers," since their duty is primarily to feed the flock (see chapter 1). However, in this section we will discuss two distinct types of workers, the "pastor" of a local church and the "teacher" at a Bible college or seminary. The one trains laymen at the local level, and the other trains the leaders who themselves will teach the local believers. Both must build upon the techniques already expounded in previous chapters, and they must employ quite distinct methods in doing so. At the same time, we wish to apply this to the "non-professional" area of the Sunday school teacher, and we will do so under "The Teacher and Tools."

The Pastor and Tools

In previous years, preaching reached a low point and there seemed to be signs of its passing; some even went so far as to celebrate its demise. However, there is evidence that it once again is growing and attaining new relevance. Nearly every church leader today notes the centrality of the pulpit. In a survey of 1,300 ministers regarding the preacher's task, preaching was voted first in importance. Interestingly, however, in the area of time spent it was fifth out of six![2]

The purpose of this chapter is to help the parish pastor to align his time with his priority list (see further the discussion of priorities in chap. 1). Time management has long been recognized as a crucial need in the efficient performance of pastors. The key is a disciplined approach involving priority lists and constant organization of one's schedule. At the top of the list must be time spent in God's Word, first and foremost as a worshiper, and then as one leading the worship of God's people. It is our opinion that preparation alone, apart from personal Bible study, must be given a minimum of twenty hours per week. To many ministers this seems impossible, but it is very possible with proper delegation of authority and tasks. There are many things which the minister should allow the congregation to do, freeing himself for the more important responsibility of feeding his flock.

The tragic lack of Bible-centered preaching in many pulpits is due to the fact that they have become program-centered or activity-centered rather than teaching-centered. At the same time there is a lack of depth in the expository preaching ministry. There are two reasons for this: (1) Ministers are unwilling to take the time for preparation (see further below) (2) They are afraid the congregation will react against it. In this latter regard, R. E. O. White lists three problems in expository preaching,[3] and we would like to answer each in order to alleviate the fears this idea may present to some.

(1) *It takes an expert to do well.* Actually, this is partially true, but it is misunderstood. Indeed, preachers are meant to be "experts" on God's Word by the very fact of their calling. But this

does not mean that they must have a detailed knowledge of every biblical passage; that is why we recommend commentaries and the like as excellent preaching tools. A disciplined approach to the preaching ministry, applying the rules of in-depth Bible study to the proclamation of Scripture, will make the average pastor the kind of "expert" he needs to be. Like all disciplines, it takes practice and hard work. But as every paragraph in this study is meant to show, the rewards are worth the effort.

(2) *It can lead to dryness, an academic approach without power or life to it.* This also is often true, and many expositors' sermonic styles have been dry and dull. However, it does not have to be so. It is unfortunate that many today force a dichotomy between style and content. Those who major in style have powerful illustrations and rhetorical application but spend little time trying to understand the text. Those who major in content spend a great deal of time explaining minute details and seemingly insignificant words but never fire the imagination. In terms of need, the content is more important, but in terms of audience reaction, style is more important. In actuality the two are interdependent, and one must use both to become a true expositor of God's Word. In this chapter we hope to show how this may be done.

(3) *It is often irrelevant, as if the preacher were speaking to a first-century audience.* Again, this need not be true. The problem is that many "scholar-preachers" neglect application, expecting their audience to do that for themselves. This is a serious error, for such an approach fails to catch the attention of the average "man-in-the-pew." Relevance must be demonstrated, not assumed. We hope to show the necessity of "life-situations" preaching, that is, the application of the biblical data to the needs of the audience. As White says, "topical sermons *appear* more relevant, at the expense of authority."[4]

Description of Expository Preaching

Technically, expository preaching is preaching from a single passage, explaining its meaning, then applying it to the congregation. As such, it is both a science and an art, applying the rules of rhetoric to the art of communication. Three elements must be united: the content, i.e., God's truth; the means, i.e., the preacher's personality and gifts; and the goal, i.e., the audience's needs. The preacher then becomes a divine messenger, forming a bridge between God's message and the congregation. As R. H. Mounce has written, "Preaching is . . . the medium through which God contemporizes His historic self-disclosure and offers man the opportunity to respond in faith."[5] The preacher then has the responsibility of making certain it is God's truth that he is communicating. The proliferation of cults today is the best illustration of the ease with which an audience may be deceived. Expository preaching is the only way to make certain that one is sticking to God's truth rather than dealing with man-made interpretations.

Of course, we do not wish to negate the possibility of topical sermons. We would accept a broad definition of "expository" preaching, that is, any message which is faithful to the message of the original autographs. A topical or doctrinal message is expository if it restricts itself to a proper exegesis of the passages expounded in it and avoids proof-texting, that is, taking passages out of context and giving them interpretations never intended by the author. At the same time, however, the strictly expository series, expounding a book or section in a series of messages, should remain the core of the pulpit ministry. Ministers must get congregations "back to the Bible," and the only way to do this adequately is to show them how to do so in a series of expository messages. An expository sermon should have the following characteristics:

(1) *Authoritative in tone.* If the minister is truly God's spokesman delivering God's message, there will be power and a sense of authority observable in the sermon itself. While prophetic preaching is technically impossible today, since no minister has a "new revelation" from God, the ministry is still prophetic, for God's Word is proclaimed anew in the message—it becomes a direct communication from God to man when illuminated by the Holy Spirit. This sovereign strength should be evident in the very tone of the sermon.

(2) *Spiritually alive.* In one sense there should be no difference between a minister's "quiet time" and his sermon preparation—a sermon should be preached first of all to himself and should meet his spiritual needs before it is proclaimed to his congregation. A minister's rule of thumb should be, Never preach a sermon which has not spoken to you. A common error of the professional is to study the Bible "third-hand," from the standpoint of a minister's audience rather than his own. But the audience needs first-hand preaching, in which they feel the excitement of spiritual truth in the very voice and manner of the preacher. This can come only when the minister himself has applied it anew to his own life before he applies it to the needs of his congregation. If the sermon does not result from the prayer closet, it should not be preached. The pastor must agonize over both his message and his audience before he delivers God's message.

(3) *Dynamic in results.* A sermon's goal must be to change lives, not just to inform. Teaching is at the heart of the pulpit ministry, but it must be made experiential as well as factual. The Bible was never intended to be a series of dogmatic traditions passed on from generation to generation. The very core of its purpose is to bring man back to God and to change lives. Thus

there is no room in a pulpit ministry for strict dogma without application to current needs. For example, the central meaning of the incarnation is not factual truth but rather dynamic experience—it is the basis of our new life in Christ (cf. Gal. 4:4–7 and Phil. 2:5–11). In preaching, the total man must be reached—the intellect, the emotions, the will—and all aspects must be transformed. Spiritual, psychological, and social needs must be met. This means, of course, that the preacher's assignment is exceedingly complex, and this is why he must restrict himself only to God's Word; it alone is sufficient for the task.

(4) *Meet people where they are.* An important need in expository preacing is "life-situation" application. Here the minister makes certain that the congregation realizes the relevance of the passage for their current situations and needs. The message will integrate the Christian message with politics, education, art, and so on. The prophetic responsibility of the pastor must lead him to address all the ills of society, and the priestly responsibility must result in showing the connection between God's promises and man's needs, tying biblical answers to specific problems today.

The reason in-depth preaching seems dry and uninteresting is not in the discipline itself but in the style of the sermon.[6] If the preacher would eschew technical terms and preach in the language and style of his people, they would respond.

Methodology for Expository Preaching

Once again, the key to good preaching is a willingness to take the time in preparation and prayer. It is unfortunate that many seem to believe that "preachers are born, not made." This is only partially true; natural gifts are a great advantage, but this fails to take into consideration spiritual gifts. When God calls a person to a task, He gives the gifts to perform it. In addition, hard work and knowledge of techniques give the gift a better chance to surface. No gifted pianist ever became a concert performer without hours, even years, of hard practice; nor does a great athlete ever win an Olympic gold medal without knowledge of advanced training techniques and theory. One must combine the two—the gift which God gives and the knowledge and practice of techniques in using His gift.

(1) *Time management.* F. D. Whitesell gives six suggestions for conserving time preparing a sermon. First, set aside certain times for preparation and keep those inviolable. Since short periods are impractical (it takes too long to get going), three to four hours at a stretch is best. Only emergencies should interrupt; if you do not have a secretary, study at home where your spouse can intercept. Also, explain the situation to the congregation so they will understand. Second, plan your sermon schedule ahead so you can collect ideas and material as they come to you. This will ensure continuity in the preaching program; we recommend keeping six months ahead in your planning. Third, begin early in the week of the message to prepare in earnest. Fourth, carry a notebook with you to record ideas; it is good to keep it handy even at night (with a reading light if you're married), since ideas that come to you then may be forgotten by morning. Fifth, maintain regular personal Bible study; it is amazing how often the Lord dovetails that with your sermonic needs. Some of the best supporting passages or illustrative material is discovered in this fashion. Sixth, build up sermonic habits. It takes literally one-fourth the amount of time to do the same work after two years or so in the ministry. A pastor can learn by previous mistakes and successes, experimenting with new techniques and methods as he goes.

(2) *The sermonic idea.* In an expository sermon, the sermonic idea is related to finding the key idea of the passage. We have

already discussed this in previous chapters so here will restrict ourselves to applying it to the sermon. It becomes the "great idea" around which the sermon is based, and the pastor dare not neglect it in favor of a peripheral theme. This does not mean he cannot focus on these other themes; rather, he must apply them to the major idea. An example may be found in preaching prophecy regarding the Lord's return, a favorite topic today. Most sermons seem to restrict themselves to the future hope, building elaborate pictures of "what will be" in the future age. However, they neglect the fact that every major passage on the parousia of the Lord relates future eschatology to present ethics, stressing that the future hope must change one's present way of living—cf. I Corinthians 15 (v. 58), II Corinthians 5 (vv. 9–10), I Thessalonians 4 (vv. 9–12), and II Peter 3 (v. 11). True preaching on the Lord's return dare not neglect this crucial aspect.

(3) *The sermon outline.* This is a third step after the preliminary and final outline already discussed in previous chapters. Here we would repeat that the sermon outline should not depart from the basic outline of the text itself. Jay Adams would say that at times the sermonic purpose and audience will determine the outline rather than the natural division of the text.[7] The danger with this is the absence of controls on truth; that is, often one will not preach Scriptural truth but rather his own truth. The two may not coincide, with the result that one preaches a half truth or no truth at all. The solution is to highlight certain aspects of the exegesis on the basis of the needs of the moment but not to change the outline or author's intention. Adams advises adapting or translating the natural divisions to the preaching situation; it is better, however, to restrict oneself to the natural division, emphasize the point which applies, and note how the rest balances and provides context for the specific point.

There are five parts to a sermon outline: title, propositional statement (purpose or goal of the sermon), introduction, body

(major and minor points), and conclusion. The Bible study outline will be adapted to the sermonic form and most of the rest of
the discussion will be devoted to methodology for successfully
accomplishing this.

(4) *Sermonic style.* One of the major differences between the
Bible study and the sermon is style. The sermon must be rhetorical rather than didactic, that is, it must be presented in language
which will interest and grip the audience. The importance of
style dare not be underestimated. As John A. Broadus has said,
"[Style] can render mediocrity acceptable and even attractive,
and power more powerful still. It can make error seductive, while
truth may lie unnoticed for want of its aid. Shall religious
teachers neglect so powerful a means of usefulness?"[8] Style is the
instrument by which a sermon becomes memorable.

Words are our tools, and the means by which the Holy Spirit
works through us. Tools never hone themselves; the creative use
of language takes hard work and diligent effort, and develops only
through constant practice. Paul in I Corinthians 2:4 seemingly
derogated this when he said, "My speech and my preaching were
not with persuasive words of man's wisdom." However, at times
his language soars with excellence. In this passage Paul actually
says that he refused to indulge in the fanciful speculative philosophy of his day; but he felt free to use the highest powers of
rhetoric in proclaiming the true and simple gospel.

First, it is important to acquire one's own style. By its very
nature, "style" is that which is characteristic of a person. This
does not mean that it must always come naturally; in fact it
usually must be developed through great exertion over a period of
time. All great writers have struggled with their styles. At the
same time, style does express the essence of what makes you, you.
Start noticing the way you phrase things and characteristically
speak. Then build on that and start working on sentence structure

and vocabulary. Learn to reword sentences several times until they have that "certain ring." For the correct words, use *Roget's Thesaurus*.

When preparing a sermon, try putting it into words instead of just forming a skeleton outline. Think through the "right way" to say each part. There are two methods: write it out in manuscript form (though we do not recommend preaching from a manuscript), for taking the time to write out a sermon helps one verbalize it; or practice preaching it and work through each sentence as you do it. Finally, pray over it note by note and phrase by phrase, allowing the Spirit to aid your choice.

There are several requirements for good style. A sermon must have clarity, and must be expressed in language which is easily understood by *your* congregation (this means sermons should be reworked for different audiences.) A common error of young seminary graduates is to use the terms they learned in school, regardless of the fact that those in their audience are unfamiliar with them.

Second, a sermon should show energy or forcefulness. Vitality is just as important in the message's construction as in its delivery. The best way to achieve this enthusiasm for a message you feel is vitally important; you must seek animate, passionate expression, appealing to the imagination through imagery and illustration. Use rhythmic, alliterative phrases, perhaps with onomatopoeia for vividness (e.g., "the syncopated popping of the campfire"). Avoid overused expressions such as "sleeping like a log" and seek the unusual expression, such as "he seemed as peaceful as the summer oak, swaying gently in the breeze."

Fluency and elegance add an air of poetry to good prose. It can be overdone, and many a preacher has failed here because he eschewed simplicity for complex, unwise elegance. True elegance magnifies rather than hides the point of the message. The key is the wise use of the imagination. Note the style of the commentaries and other works as you read them, and study imaginative literature (poetry, drama, fiction) as well as the works of the great preachers. Learn to think in terms of impressions—what will reach both the eyes and the ears of the members of the audience you are addressing.[8] Paint pictures which will capture their imagination and drive your point home. Imaginative prose dare not obscure the point, but must motivate the listener in the direction of your sermonic goal.

(5) *The introduction.* It is important to catch the attention of the audience and set the mood for the sermon. The introduction should follow the exegesis so it can be tailored to the final thrust, that is, the propositional statement which proclaims the goal of the sermon. There should be one major goal of each sermon, and it is the job of the introduction to propose and illustrate this in such a way that the audience becomes intrigued and prepared to listen to the development of this idea in the body of the sermon.

Lloyd M. Perry points to three parts of a good introduction.[9] First, the *approach sentence* is based on the key idea and leads into the introduction proper. It should be dynamic and fluent. For example, a sermon based on the proposition, "fulfill our spiritual obligations" (Heb. 10:19–25) may begin, "Have any of you ever been in debt?" Second, the *introduction proper* must be brief (approximately 10 percent of the sermon) and catchy. It dare not be too complex and should lead into the discourse itself. We prefer a secular introduction, starting with some area common to the daily life of your audience (such as debt!) and leading them to the spiritual proposition. Third, the *transition* to the body of the sermon bridges from the secular introduction to the biblical proposition and presents the propositional statement which is to be developed.

(6) *The body of the sermon.* Here one works with the notes of the Bible study and reworks them along the lines of the propo-

sitional statement. The major points are expressed in more popular form, so that the audience can easily remember them. For example, the Bible study outline of Hebrews 10:19-25 would have three main points: (1) Confidently draw near to God in worship (vv. 19-22); (2) Hold fast the confession of our hope (v. 23); and (3) Consider how to stimulate one another to love and good works (vv. 24-25). The sermon itself will focus on Christian obligations and will simplify the outline by pointing out that it progresses from our obligation to God (point 1) to our obligation to man (point 3, with point 2 relating to both) and rephrasing the points thusly: (1) Obligation to worship; (2) Obligation to confess; (3) Obligation to help one another.

Transitions between points are a difficult part of any sermon outline. Properly, numbers are given only to main points. If you number subpoints as well, you are apt to confuse your audience. The only exception is in a teaching sermon, and then only if the outline is either in the bulletin or on an overhead transparency. If the outline is done properly, transitions should be natural and easy. In reality, however, transitions are often the hardest part of the sermon to do well. There are three aspects to a good transition: The summary of a past section ("We have seen that Jesus taught that God's forgiveness is based on our forgiving attitude"); a transitional phrase ("now"); and the lead into the next section ("let us see how the epistles develop this theme"). The key is brevity and simplicity.

(7) *The conclusion.* There are several purposes for a conclusion. It sums up the message, drives its point home, and motivates the audience to act on it. It should be slightly shorter than the introduction, because the congregation is not prepared for an elaborate discourse after sitting through the sermon proper. Therefore it should consist of concise, well-phrased sentences with a personal appeal. Every person should feel it is addressed specifically to him. It should be phrased in positive terms, telling

the audience what to do rather than what to avoid; this is psychologically the superior appeal. Finally, it should be forceful, direct and urgent; every person should leave feeling he must act on the demands of the message.

(8) *Illustrations.* These are crucial because they make the points understandable and meaningful to the audience. Illustrations should explain the point (the literal meaning of the term is "to throw light" on the subject), attract attention, arouse emotions (an important motivational tool), give relief by introducing a light aspect in a serious discussion, and help the audience remember the point. In fact, it is often true that the listener remembers the illustration far longer than the point itself. For this reason it is very important that the illustration be carefully geared to teach the point.

There are many sources for good illustrations. Of course, there are the books on sermon illustrations, some of which are good, but more often than not they do not meet your need exactly. The best sources are observation from life itself and personal experience. Life provides a fascinating backdrop for illustrations— nature and science can give details which prove very interesting (as in the Moody science films); business procedures, social problems, and national or cultural idiosyncracies can provoke great interest. Travel is a broadening experience, especially time spent getting to know other cultures (the preacher might consider trading pulpits for a year with someone in England or Scotland, for instance). Personal illustrations put you on the level of the congregation and create empathy. This is one of our favorite sources. Other sources are the Bible (one of the best, since the stories are theological in their essence), literature, newspapers, and magazines (current events can be very meaningful and *Reader's Digest*, to name one, abounds with hundreds of possibilities). It is a viable practice to set up an illustration file, numbered under each subject and corss-referenced (e.g., "see interpersonal relationship #33"), since some illustrations would apply to several areas. If you do so, avoid choosing "favorites" which are used over and over in various sermons; one way is to note on the filed item when and where it has been used (e.g., "Heb. 10:19–25" sermon, 9/17/78). Finally, we might note that some of the best illustrations come out of your Bible study. The cultural or historical background behind a passage can be fascinating and helps to illuminate the meaning of the statement.

(9) *Application.* The Bible is above all a personal book, meant to be applied in one's own life. However, application must be secondary to preparation, for one must first discover what the text means before he can apply it. At the same time, the truth itself is an "I–thou" summons from God to the individual, meant to be lived in his life. The preacher must separate the timeless truth from the temporary application, basing the latter on the former. Further application should not be restricted to the conclusion but should be found at every point of the message.

The major purpose is to focus the truth on your audience's personal needs, drawing their attention to the way it applies today. This may be done through inference (direct lessons from the passage), illustration (indirect life-situational suggestions), or practical implications (showing the "how" as well as the "what" of the sermon idea, an area unfortunately neglected in many sermons). It is important to maintain a pastor's heart of love as you do this, for it is easy to degenerate into a browbeating style of confrontation. Unless led by the Spirit, the latter seldom changes lives.

(10) *Motivation and persuasion.* There are three stages in attaining results from a sermon: the points are applied, the congregation is persuaded about the truth proclaimed, then it is motivated to put that truth into practice. Persuasion cannot be

accomplished in a moment, and it is a common error for preachers to expect instantaneous acquiescence to their arguments. Rather, a preacher should take his time and lead people to agreement slowly, showing empathy for the trauma he is causing them. He should try not to take on too much and thereby fail to make his point. In important areas, such as doctrinal error or unconfessed sin, it is best to work over a period of time, leading the congregation to the goal via a series of messages, each building on the other. The preacher must know his topic, formulate it carefully, and honestly consider all sides in answering opponents. He must think through his interpretation and check his facts, logic, the reliability of his sources, and coherence.[10]

The motivation must build on the content (truth) and persuasion (argument). It normally involves an appeal to the will or emotions. The speaker endeavors to show how the sermon idea will help to fulfill the listeners' basic needs or desires and thereby motivates them to do something about it. Here we must caution the reader to proceed very carefully, for motivational research has shown that a persuasive appeal to the basic drives can force people to do literally anything. Therefore a hyperemotional appeal can produce false, temporary results and could be a breach of ethics. A balanced approach, however, is important, and in this age of sophistication is almost expected by the average audience. The balance between the emotional and the logical[11] is a difficult but necessary element of a good sermon.

The key is emotive language, which calls for action and leads the people to act upon the point made. However, the preacher must be careful to keep his truth content secure. He may speak positively and glowingly about the results of the desired action, but he must be certain that the results are biblically based. Hyperbole is a common problem in the motivational part of a sermon, and this tendency must be carefully considered when preparing a sermon. Since the emotive achieves results, it is easy for a speaker to begin replacing content with emotion; then he or she is in danger of destroying the eternal relevance to obtain temporary results.

Summary. The preacher must use all the tools at his disposal to meet his primary responsibility—"feeding the flock" in his charge (John 21:15–17; Eph. 4:1–12; I Peter 5:2–4). At the heart of the sermonic process is a detailed exegesis of the passage(s) upon which the message is based. While this is a great privilege, it still takes much discipline to spend the four hours or so each day necessary to a proper pulpit/teaching ministry.

After the passage has been studied in depth, the minister reworks it along the lines of his audience's needs (life-situation), decides· which aspects to highlight, and adds the illustrations, application, and motivation. The final step, then, is to deliver the message. Here it is important to be relaxed yet enthusiastic, to be articulate and confident in one's presentation, to use variety in pitch, inflection, pace, and volume, to be animated in both vocal tone and gestures, to maintain good eye contact, to use facial expressions to establish the changing emotions of the message. This will produce in the audience a confidence in the preacher's sincerity and a hunger for the truth which he bears to them as God's messenger. All of these are important tools, yet all are dependent and must build only upon the study of God's Word, which is the true foundation of the message's relevance. The other tools are merely instruments, and must be subservient to the overriding task of involving the audience in God's revelation to them.

Finally, we might note that the average pastor stresses content over methodology. That is, he tells what the Bible says but rarely gets around to telling the congregation how he discovered this, or how they can discover similar insights in Scripture and apply it for themselves. Part of the fault lies with the system itself, for we have retreated back into a semi-medieval stance where proclamation has precedence over dialogue and where the minister seems to be the only church member with enough "expertise" to interpret the Bible. This will change only when church attitudes change in this regard. If the pastor is to fulfill his responsibility as "teacher" (Eph. 4:11), he must teach "how" as well as "what." Since this will be discussed in greater depth in the next section, the pastor is encouraged to apply the points there to himself as well.

The Teacher and Tools

Here we must note two categories of teacher, each with distinct needs and each with differing levels of preparation. Their task, however, is identical—helping God's people learn to use Scripture and to make it practical in their lives. These two kinds of teachers are the Sunday school teacher and the teacher in the Christian school.

The Sunday school teacher. The teacher in a primary or junior class may feel that this study hardly relates to him. However, we would make two points in this regard: (1) Deep Bible study is an obligation for every Christian in fulfilling God's will and calling; therefore, to keep spiritually alert, all teachers should be engaged in the type of approach described in this handbook. (2) There needs to be more emphasis in the lower grades on Bible study. In our public schools the children are progressively taught how to learn and why it is important. We need a similar approach in our churches; while Bible stories and flannelgraph lessons are meaningful, children can be taught the "ABC's" of Bible study, too. There is a need for quality books similar to second grade history readers, and the like, to be used to prepare children and encourage their desire to study Scripture. This will bear fruit later as maturing young people are introduced to detailed Bible study.

With the growing realization of the importance of adult education in the local church, the work of the Sunday school teacher takes on even more significance. It is at this level that an in-depth approach is essential. The adult Sunday school teacher should be practiced in the art of Bible study. While he or she will often not have Bible college or seminary training, this by no means restricts him or her so long as there is a willingness to read and study.

In an early class the teacher can go through works such as Oletta Wald's *Joy of Discovery* or Robert Traina's *Methodical Bible Study*, then through a book such as this. Next the class can begin doing book studies using commentaries, perhaps beginning with Genesis or Amos in the Old Testament and John or James in the New Testament (while John is one of the first books to recommend to the new convert, it is one of the most difficult for deep Bible study due to the advanced theological concepts it contains; therefore it might be easier to start with Mark or Matthew.) The class may also begin with some of the excellent inductive study guides (those which deal with studying the text alone without other study aids) and then add the more detailed commentary study in subsequent quarters. The main principle is to lead the class (and yourself!) slowly into the difficult, time-consuming, but extremely rewarding world of in-depth Bible study. It is important to teach the class members not only what the text says, but how they can discover these truths for themselves. In this regard the Sunday school teacher would do well to read the next section below, since most of those principles will apply to them.

The professional teacher. The so-called "professional" Bible teacher in the college or seminary has often had a quite different education background from the pastor. It is amazing how few have had pastoral experience and how many have almost a purely academic interest/approach in their teaching. Many of these teachers can *do* useful research for themselves, but few teach *how* to do research in the classroom. Many are scholars more than teachers and give out content rather than methodology in the classroom. This is a serious error. The reason many pastors seldom use Greek or Hebrew in their sermon preparation is not only due to the problem of time; it is unfortunately also because they have never been shown the tremendous relevance of the original languages for the pulpit ministry. Biblical courses are often too academic in their approach; somehow there must be a balance between content and methodology. Several ideas for achieving this are as follows:

(1) *Motivate the student.* A definite P. R. (public relations) approach is needed in the classroom. Motivation techniques need to be employed when one teaches a biblical course. The most important technique is the teacher's own excitement regarding the relevance of the truths he is teaching. Students desire relevant courses; a common complaint in all disciplines (even engineering or medicine) is that the professor has never left the classroom (i.e., theory) for the practical laboratory of life (i.e., application). The gap is never bridged and the student has little to apply when he, in turn, becomes teacher and cannot simply assume that he has his students' attention. As Kenneth Eble says, the teacher

expends intelligence and imagination in trying to establish relationships between what he is trying to teach and whatever the students know and value. Other things being equal, the higher the relevance for the student, the more effective the teaching.[12]

At the same time, the content must be stressed. In many ways, it possesses its own relevance. If the classes are no more than a series of sermons, the student will never be motivated to study seriously the biblical material. Application, in both sermons and Bible courses, can easily replace depth. However, as the teacher goes into a passage in depth, he can show the student how the data could be used as a sermon illustration.

For example, one of the best sermons on prayer can be preached from the Lord's Prayer, Matthew 6:9–13. Here one can note the Jewish background of the prayer, as in the first two "thou-petitions" (the sermon would be based on the two kinds of petitions—worship or "thou-petitions," and supplication or "we-petitions"). "May your kingdom come" is intimately connected to "May your name be made holy" in the Jewish *Kaddish* prayer which closed the synagogue service. The rabbis had a saying, "Any prayer in which the kingdom is never mentioned is no true prayer."[13] God's name will truly be made holy only when His kingdom has come. The application can then be made to our own prayer life and desire for Jesus' return. Also, the teacher can point out that the Lord's Prayer is far more than a Jew praying the *Kaddish*; in Christ the kingdom has already entered this age, as is shown in the theme of the following petition, "Your will be done on earth, as in heaven." However, the application must be carefully controlled in a teaching situation; it is better to teach the students how to apply the content. A judicious use of example to illustrate how to apply the data is the best motivation possible.

Another motivation is to communicate that learning is pleasure. When one recognizes the pure joy of discovering truth, detailed study becomes easy. Of course, before we can teach this, we have to discover it ourselves. Herein lies the importance of an in-depth devotional life for the teacher. As we begin to realize how many truths are locked into each phrase of Scripture, our enthusiasm is communicated to our students.

Other techniques are found in Eble's discussion of eight keys to effectiveness in teaching:

a. *Discipline.* One must consider all aspects of teaching and the learning experience. He must constantly test methods to see which work best.
b. *Generosity.* This must be exhibited toward both the students and the content of their classes. It is not true that the best teacher is the one who makes his classes the hardest.
c. *Energy.* Both physically (voice and gesture) and mentally (development and argumentation), the teacher must project a vigorous image to the student.
d. *Variety.* Break the lecture into segments and pace the style and delivery to fit the needs of the class and the subject.
e. *Illustrate.* Use imagination to demonstrate the class material. Translate learning into doing by applying the content to the student's life.
f. *Enthusiasm.* Project excitement about both the subject matter and the student's learning experience.
g. *Clarity and organization.* Organize the course from the student's perspective rather than your own. Help him to understand how all the information in the course fits together.
h. *Honesty.* Be willing to admit when you do not know or are wrong. Project an image that the student can trust, a moral standard that says you care about truth and error, about right and wrong.[14]

(2) *Spend time showing how to do research.* The teacher should demonstrate how he has derived his content as well as presenting the content in class. For example, for one class period he could distribute commentaries and reference works, and show how to use material and come to conclusions. He could also show how to use the class material to prepare a sermon or give a Bible study.

One important point would be to illustrate how to simplify the in-depth material for laymen. Few lay people have any difficulty with thorough Bible study, provided it is presented simply and interestingly. The students must be shown how to translate the data of the course into their own methodology, that is, how to do it themselves in their own Bible study and pulpit ministry.

In addition, the teacher must show the students that he cares not only about the subject matter but also about them as individuals. He must not only impart truth; he must prepare lives. Therefore, he must be willing to spend time with students, get to know them, and share his life with them. Academic conversation should be integrated with general social discussion. The separation of the two in most educational institutions is a harmful dichotomy which will continue to hamper a student's learning the rest of his life. Students tend to place their professors in an "ivory tower" world and so find it easy to separate academics from their general needs. A professor must show students that he has a well-rounded life and that academics has an important place in their own integrated lives.

(3) *Use term paper projects wisely.* Give the student a variety of learning experiences and make each as practical as possible. Research papers are an excellent learning experience. The heart of biblical research is exegetical study of selected passages, preferably of short portions so the student can realize how much depth there is.[15] Future papers (they should follow the exegetical study and be based on exegesis) could center on a series of exegetical sermon outlines, biblical theology (tracing a theme through a single book), or notes for teaching a class or church group.

In systematic theology, students can be encouraged to use creative methods in presenting doctrines and interacting with issues.[16] The same creative techniques can be encouraged in advanced homiletics and practical seminars. In this, though, we must be careful to stress that content must be the center of the project. Creativity must never be allowed to replace depth (as it too often does); it should be used only to teach the message clearly and better involve the audience.[17]

(4) *Offer a course in research methods and writing techniques.* This course is often neglected entirely and is seldom required of everyone; however, it is too important to be left for only a few. Many students never learn the methodology and thrill of research. Moreover, students are required to write term papers in college and seminary and should be shown how to do so properly. The problem is that students assume such courses are dry and academic, for the tremendous relevance of library research and background material in the search for truth has not been communicated to them. Such a course should include writing style, the proper use of language, and the use of imagery to strengthen a formal study. Though this parallels English classes, the course should specialize in formal writing style.

(5) *Use faculty chapels to illustrate the value of thorough Bible study.* When a faculty member preaches, he becomes an example to the student, for the purpose of his content classes is to prepare the student to proclaim the truths of Scripture. Therefore he has a sacred obligation to preach an in-depth, well-developed expository message. The instructor must avoid the temptation to preach a hurriedly-prepared message centering on illustration rather than content. The student will always emulate the examples he has seen. How many of us can honestly echo Paul's words in Philippians 3:17, "Be imitators of me, brethren, and be careful that you walk even as you have us for an example"? We must consider the implications of this for our own responsibility as teachers.[18]

(6) *Show that there are answers to critical problems.* It is very easy for a teacher to avoid critical problems, thinking that they

have no relevance to practical situations. This is often due to a misunderstanding of presuppositional apologetics, for many proceed on the basis of proclaiming the Word alone rather than dealing with apologetic issues. This neglects the fact that nearly all the well-known presuppositionalists, such as Cornelius Van Til, Gordon Clark, Francis Schaeffer, or John Whitcomb devote a great deal of their writing to apologetics, answering the critiques of non-evangelicals.

If professors avoid such critical problems, students will not know that answers exist, and they will have no answers when such questions arise in their ministries. This approach ignores the fact that many liberals in modern churches are hungry for truth, and would listen to evangelical answers. Apologetics has been too long neglected in our schools, and should be presented as a valid option to academically-inclined students looking for a way to use their gift. The Lord has opened many doors in recent years, and we must be careful to walk through each one. Of course, this subject can be overemphasized, and many teachers seem to do little more than deal with critical issues in their classes. Practical exegesis and critical apologetics must be kept in balance.

(7) *Use methods other than pure lecture.*[19] Most studies in educational theory conclude that the lecture method is one of the poorest for involving the student in the learning experience. It is crucial to teach these developing minds to think rather than merely to record and memorize data. One valuable way to do this is called the "discursive method." This means that the teacher seeks to draw the student into the subject through strategic questions, discussion, and the wise use of rhetorical devices. In the long run, we could even go so far as to say that content is not as important as motivation and methodology.[20] Of course, this goal cannot be accomplished unless the course does contain the content, but our main objective is to teach the student how to teach

in the future, not just to give him good class notes to use on that particular subject.

Some suggestions for putting this to practical use are as follows: (1) Have students teach a class as their project; (2) have the whole class prepare class notes on a series of sermons and then meet in seminar once a week to discuss problems; (3) have the professor's class notes mimeographed and spend the class time clarifying, discussing methodology, and so forth.

(8) *Establish a standard of excellence in your school.* Professors must constantly stress the biblical teaching regarding the proper use of one's gifts and talents. If professors—and students—do not develop those gifts to the best of their ability, they will be held accountable to God. This does not mean that the school should create a high pressure situation where everyone competes for grades. Competition and grades are not important; rather, a school must create a dynamic atmosphere where everyone seeks to do his best. Schools must begin to teach that grades *per se* are not the most important aspect of education. Studies[21] have shown that later success is not correlated with grade-point average. Rather, it is the discipline and learning techniques developed which have determined success. It is far better to be a C student working hard for B— grades than to be an A student lazily earning B+ grades.

If a professor can motivate the student to seek excellence in the use of his gifts, he has accomplished his purpose. Of course, this also means that he dare not allow himself to do a mediocre job in the classroom. His purpose is not to please the students but to challenge and teach them. Both content and methodology must be of the highest quality, and the professor must put a lot of prayer and effort into his classroom performance.

(9) *Stress the professional development of the faculty in your*

school. Many critics decry the emphasis of Ph.D. or Th.D. degrees, for the degrees themselves are based on research ability rather than on teaching competence. This is valid, but we must note the danger that after earning degrees, many teachers return to speak far above their pupils' level of understanding. In other words, the academic degree has hurt their classroom communication more than it has helped. Nevertheless, when the problems are recognized and countered, the further degrees are a definite advantage in that they strengthen the scholarly ability of the teacher.

However, our primary meaning of "professional development" is in the area of teaching methodology. Again, a proper balance must be kept between academic research and teaching. A professor's primary responsibility is to teach students to the best of his ability; his secondary privilege is to share his gifts with a wider audience outside the confines of the school.

Under the first category, schools must begin to educate the faculty with regard to teaching theory and practice. All teachers need to keep abreast of valid alternatives in teaching technique. There needs to be an atmosphere of experimentation, that is, trying new ways to involve the student better in the learning process. Under the second category, schools need to place greater stress on academic achievement and research competence in the faculty. This can be done by lightening the teaching (six hours per semester is preferable, nine hours is maximum) and extracurricular load of teachers (e.g., administrative or P. R. duties) and by a workable sabbatical policy which encourages writing. These two methods would help establish a balance between teaching and research in the faculty. In conclusion, we might note that professors cannot produce students of the Word until they become such themselves.

Conclusion

In-depth Bible study, as we have seen, is meant for every believer, whether a lay student of the Word or a professional Christian worker. The preacher and teacher, in the latter category, have a special responsibility to fulfill and must be careful to maintain the high standards that God requires of them. We must remember that God does not require us to be brilliant, but He does require us to be faithful. Spending an extensive amount of time in detailed study of Scripture does not take a genius, but it does take a disciplined believer. Faithfulness and discipline are two sides of the same coin.

In this chapter the preacher and the teacher have been shown practical ways to achieve their goal, to develop disciples who learn at the feet of their Master (the definition of discipleship). There is no greater purpose, and the reward is found in the act itself. "And the things you have heard me say in the presence of many witnesses entrust to reliable men who will also be qualified to teach others" (II Tim. 2:2, NIV).

Notes

1. In the original Greek of this verse, "pastors and teachers" refers to a single office rather than two distinct offices.

2. See H. C. Brown, Jr., et al., *Steps to the Sermon* (Nashville: Broadman Press, 1963), pp. 10–11, for a more detailed discussion. The minister was felt to be primarily (1) a preacher, (2) a pastor, (3) a priest, (4) a teacher, (5) an organizer, (6) an administrator. However, in actual time spent in these tasks, the order was no. 6, no. 2, no. 3, no. 5, no. 1, no. 4.

3. R. E. O. White, *A Guide to Preaching* (Grand Rapids: Eerdmans, 1973), pp. 23–24.

4. Ibid., p. 24, italics mine.

5. R. H. Mounce, *The Essential Nature of New Testament Preaching* (Grand Rapids: Eerdmans, 1960), p. 153.

6. A good discussion may be found in Lloyd M. Perry, *Biblical Preaching for Today's World* (Chicago: Moody Press, 1973), chap. 5, "Biblical Preaching and Life-Situation Preaching."

7. Jay Adams, *Pulpit Speech* (Nutley, N.J.: Presbyterian and Reformed, 1971), p. 99. Adams is correct in his discussion of poetry and parables, which certainly cannot be preached in a rigid grammatical outline. However, the impression he creates that this approach can be applied to any type of biblical passage can lead to problems.

8. John A. Broadus, *A Treatise on the Preparation and Delivery of Sermons* (New York: Harper, 1944), p. 225.

9. Perry, *Biblical Preaching*, pp. 57–58.

10. For further study, see Perry, chap. 8 and Adams, chap. 4.

11. Both Broadus and Adams point out that the ignorant are too dependent on the former and the sophisticated are too dependent on the latter.

12. Kenneth E. Eble, *Professors as Teachers* (San Francisco: Jossey-Bass, 1973), p. 79. On p. 82, he adds, "Teachers must recognize that students often are not in the teacher's orbit, and that the worth and relevance of a subject do not disclose themselves in the course packaging. Finding and helping the students establish relationships between academic learning and things which matter to them is the very essence of teaching."

13. This can be found in Joachim Jeremias' classic work, *The Prayers of Jesus* (London: SCM, 1967), p. 98.

14. Eble, *Professors as Teachers*, pp. 36–53. A good example of this last point is the critique in *Sports Illustrated* (three articles, May, 1976) that the Christian athletic movements care only about converting the athletes and not about correcting the ethical sins of modern athletics. While parts of the articles exaggerate the situation, the basic criticism is well founded and shows us that our ethics must be complete as Christians. We dare not stress only one aspect of the Christian life and ignore others.

15. A good illustration of the depth of Scripture is what occurred when a first-year class was asked to do a ten-page paper on a passage not to exceed three verses. At first the students refused to believe so much could be written about so few verses. However, only one student kept it to ten pages (the rest of the class wrote more than twelve pages) and everyone asked that future classes be asked to do more than one paper.

16. For example, they could present a dialogue on the three "rapture" positions, or a debate on Calvinism vs. Arminianism. They could use flash cards, drama, or cartoons on an overhead projector to illustrate such debated doctrines as eschatology or church government.

17. The true purpose of creativity is not sensation or titillation; we are not ministering to entertain. We use it solely to help our congregation assimilate the biblical truths. For example, drama enables the listener to identify *himself* with

the point of the message; it is no longer a static doctrine but a dynamic, life-involving principle.

18. We might also mention here James 3:1, "Be not many of you teachers, my brothers, knowing that *we* will receive the greater condemnation." The changes of pronoun here shows that James includes himself in this category. The teacher is held responsible for the development of his pupils and is judged accordingly.

19. This does not mean the lecture method is outmoded or meaningless, for it is still the best way to impart content. But the lecture must be supplemented by other methods which better involve the students in thinking for themselves.

20. One important recent work challenging the value of pure content courses is Ohmer Milton, *Alternatives to the Traditional* (San Francisco: Jossey-Bass, 1973). He points (pp. 27–32) to the many experiments which show that "transfer of learning," that is, the application of data from one field to another, does not occur automatically. Rote memorization of class notes is no guarantee that the content has been made practical and usable to the student.

21. See Milton, *Alternatives*, pp. 43f.

8

Conclusion

The story is told about an amateur architect who designed his own home and ordered the builder to follow the plans without making the slightest deviation. The man then left on vacation with the parting stern reminder to the builder not to alter the plans in any way whatever. Unfortunately, the fellow had forgotten to draw in stairs for the second and third stories. By the time he returned the irate builder had long since decided to follow orders to the ludicrous letter. When the architect returned, there stood his three-story dream home with no stairway from floor to floor.

No doubt many wish a second or third story to their Christian lives and are honestly dissatisfied to live at ground level mediocrity. But unfortunately, without steps the best goal remains but a rather dangerous illusion, dangerous because it ultimately breeds frustration. In the previous chapters, we have attempted to provide some simple steps with regard to Bible study which hopefully will lead to a more "elevated" certainty (faith) of those things God has provided for us in Christ. A definiteness in procedure (chapters 2–4) and also a humility to be assisted by the tools and men which God provides (chapters 5–7), we believe, will go a long way to provide a "stairway" to one's desire to walk with God and to be of effective service to His world.

Finally, we would like to add a practical point. We who are pastors and seminary professors often make the error of taking too idealistic an approach to our expectations regarding those in our flock. In our "ivory tower" we forget the enormous pressures on the average parishioner's time. A recent article in the Trinity Evangelical Divinity School *Voices* discussed the advisability of pastors getting experience at secular jobs. In it M. Hadley Robinson said:

... my business experience has acquainted me with the everyday problems of lay men and women. Few pastors understand why parishioners are not always eager to attend church on weeknights, pursue extensive home Bible studies or participate in door-to-door evangelization. Very often the person employed in the business world comes home and barely has enough strength to open the front door! In essence, an average Christian's lack of interest in church activities may simply be the result of sheer exhaustion, not diminished sainthood. [1]

We who are "shepherds" must not *expect* our flock to take time to study the Bible; we must *motivate* them to do so. Many former pastors admit that they now have as much difficulty as any layman in getting to prayer meeting. Therefore, the Christian leader must project an aura of excitement with regard to deep Bible study. The only way to do that is to get excited ourselves, and then share with our congregation the reasons why we are excited. The great task for today is producing men and women of the Word, Christian workers whose fellowship and ministry reflect the one truly relevant Book of the ages!

Notes

1. M. Hadley Robinson, "Thanks, Dr. Perry!" in *Voices*, Trinity Evangelical Divinity School, IV no. 2 (Feb, 1978), p. 9.

Appendix

Out-of-Print
Book Sources

USED BOOK DEALERS

Used book lists can be obtained from the following on a regular basis upon request.

North America

Alec R. Allenson, Box 31, Naperville, IL 60540.

Baker Book House, Used Book Division, 1019 Wealthy St., S.E., Grand Rapids, MI 49506.

Christian Used Book Exchange, 6943 Grange Court, Cincinnati, OH 45239.

John Nathan Stroud, Bookseller, R.D.2, Box 524, Newmanstown, PA 17073.

Kregel Publications, Used Book Division, 525 Eastern Ave., S.E., Grand Rapids, MI 49501.

Noah's Book Attic, Stoney Point, Rt. 2, Greenwood, SC 49646.

Richard Owen Roberts, Bookseller, 205 East Kehoe Blvd., Wheaton, IL 60187.

Stevens Book Shop, Corner of North & Main St., P.O. Box 71, Wake Forest, NC 27587.

The Theological Book Center, 99 Brattle St. Cambridge, MA 02138.

Europe

Antiquariatt Spinoza, Den Texstraat 26, Amsterdam, Netherlands.

B. H. Blackwell, LTD., 50 Broad St., Oxford, England OX1 3BQ.

Emerald Isle Books, 539 Antrim Rd., Belfast 15, N. Ireland BT15 3BU.

Holleyman & Son, 59 Carlisle Rd., Hove, Sussex, England BN3 4FQ.

Howes Bookshop, 3 Trinity St., Hastings, Sussex, England TN34 1HQ.

James Thin, 53–59 South Bridge, Edinburgh, Scotland EH1 1YS.

T. Wever, Boekhandel, Franeker, Netherlands.

Used book dealer directories are available at most major libraries. Among the most important of such directories are the following:

Book Dealers, European: A Directory of Dealers in Secondhand and Antiquarian Books on the Continent of Europe. London: Sheppard Press, Ltd., P.O. Box 42, 15 James St., London, England WC2E 8BX.

Book Dealers in North America. London: Sheppard Press Ltd.

A Directory of Dealers in Secondhand and Antiquarian Books in the British Isles. London: Sheppard Press Ltd.

Lewis, Roy H. *The Book Browser's Guide: Britain's Secondhand and Antiquarian Bookshops.* London: David and Charles (Holdings) Ltd., Brunel House, Newton Abbot, Devon TQ12 2DW.